Table of Contents

Foreword

Matt Ridley is in the vanguard of one of the greatest intellectual battles of our time, a battle which will eventually determine the kind of society in which we live. On the surface it is a conflict between two visions of the environment: whether it is best managed by private or by public means. But the issues raised under the banner of environmentalism are so fundamental and so numerous, and the contrast in approaches is so stark that the whole debate goes right to the heart of how we want to order our lives and our societies.

It is an old battle dressed up in new 'green' clothes. On the one side there are the *dirigiste* central planners pursuing top-down command-and-control initiatives. To them the private sector is an anathema, always and everywhere the culprit, and the solution to every problem is a mix of regulation, prohibition or even outright confiscation. Indeed, they go much further, asking 'which industries, markets and/or products . . . might be targeted for abandonment . . .?' (p. 57).

Against these misnamed 'mainstream environmentalists', Dr Ridley is a leader among a growing number of environmentalists around the world who take a different view. *First*, they question the science that lies behind the constant barrage of reports of global apocalypse and show how the funding pressures faced by scientists and lobbying groups lead to wildly inaccurate and misleading interpretations of the data.

Second, their approach emphasises:

- local initiatives and the harnessing of local knowledge;
- the fundamental rôle of private property rights to avoid the tragedy of the commons;
- the market as a discovery process;
- stewardship, incentives and responsibility;
- the role of vested interests and the effects of subsidies; and
- the incentives faced by the bureaucracy.

In other words, they advocate a decentralised, bottom-up, privately driven approach.

5

This volume brings together a selection of 30 of Dr Ridley's 'Down to Earth' columns which appear every week on the back page of the main section of *The Sunday Telegraph*. They have been grouped into six main topic areas. The columns are as originally written by Dr Ridley and so in some cases differ slightly from the published versions.

Underlying all of his articles – not just the selection presented here – is a deep concern for the environment, combined with an interdisciplinary approach which blends history, politics and economics with ornithology, climatology and forestry studies, to mention just six of the many fields with which he is familiar.

The views expressed in this IEA publication are those of the author, not of the Institute (which has no corporate view), its Trustees, Directors or Advisers. It is published as a contribution to the debate on how best to protect the environment.

February 1995   JOHN BLUNDELL
General Director, Institute of Economic Affairs

Acknowledgements

These *Down to Earth* columns are reproduced with the kind permission of *The Sunday Telegraph*.

                                                                    J.B.

The Author

Matt Ridley was born in 1958 near Newcastle-upon-Tyne. After taking BA and DPhil degrees in Zoology at the University of Oxford, and working on three wildlife conservation projects in the Indian subcontinent, he joined *The Economist* in 1983 as science correspondent. In 1984 he was made science editor, in 1987 Washington correspondent and in 1990 American editor. He was later short-listed for the post of editor.

In 1992 he moved to Northumberland where he is a freelance writer. His weekly column, 'Down to Earth', appears in *The Sunday Telegraph*, and he has also written for *The Times, Country Life, New Scientist, Esquire, Wall Street Journal, Washington Post, Newsweek, Atlantic Monthly, Science* and other newspapers and magazines.

Matt Ridley's books include *Warts and All: The Men Who Would Be Bush* (Viking, 1989) and *The Red Queen: Sex and the Evolution of Human Nature* (Penguin, 1993). The latter was short-listed for the Rhone Poulenc prize for science books and the Writers' Guild award for non-fiction books. His next book, on the evolution of human co-operation, *The Origin of Virtue*, is due out in 1996.

His wife is a lecturer at the University of Newcastle upon Tyne and they have one son.

PART I

APOCALYPSES

1. Catastrophes and Cataclysms*

Now that the Maastricht Treaty has at last come into force, I can reveal a startling fact, stranger than the strangest fiction, more spine-tingling than anything written by Nostradamus. The very last part of the age of the dinosaurs, the few million years leading up to their explosive and sudden extinction, has been for many years known to geologists as – I promise I am not making this up – the Maastrichtian period.

In the geological column, the 'upper Maastrichtian' stage of the Cretaceous era, named after a particular kind of limestone found near the infamous Belgian town, ends abruptly all over the world with what are known as boundary deposits, which are apparently the debris of a vast and global cataclysm. Virtually no scientist now disputes the idea that the age of the dinosaurs ended with a bang rather than a whimper, and most believe that the bang was caused by a collision between the earth and a very large asteroid, or possibly a comet.

Indeed, some scientists are now sure they know exactly where the object landed: on the tip of the Yucatan Peninsula in Mexico, where a crater 100 miles across lies submerged beneath limestone deposits. The creation of such a dent must have released the energy and destructive power equivalent to 5,000 Hiroshimas.

While it would be unfair from this to impute any sinister motives to the Eurocrats who planned the Maastricht summit, it is a reminder of how curiously interested in catastrophes modern science has become in recent years. This has partly reversed the great triumph of 19th-century geology and biology, its demonstration that unimaginably vast effects can flow from normal and gradual processes, given sufficient time.

Charles Lyell showed how even the deepest valleys could be carved by erosion, and that fossil shells on mountain tops were evidence not of Noah's flood but of gradual uplifting that is still going on so slowly it cannot be perceived. Charles Darwin did the same for biology with his assertion that given infinitesimally

*Published as 'A good disaster is better than an insufferable wait' in *The Sunday Telegraph* on 7 November 1993.

slow mutations and agonisingly gradual selection, a bacterium could look like a man after 600 million years.

This 'uniformitarian' revolution bred a profound distrust among scientists for any explanations that did not rely on processes that are still going on around us: for biblical floods or special creation events. Yet suddenly, in this premillennial age, the boot is on the other foot. After struggling for years to be heard, the voice of catastrophism is back. Mass extinctions, such as those that exterminated the dinosaurs, are now routinely attributed to cosmic collisions, the evidence for which is now overwhelmingly convincing.

Other sudden, destructive events have been uncovered, though not without vigorous rearguard action by uniformitarians. Most surprising of all, floods are back. In the Pacific Northwest of America, along the valley of the Columbia river, there are the geological scars of floods so vast they left gravel ripples 40 feet high. It seems that from about 15,000 years ago, for over 2,000 years, a glacier in Montana kept damming a valley and then breaking up under the force of water behind it, releasing a flood 10 times as big as all the world's rivers combined, which rushed to the sea with the energy of 200 Hiroshimas.

The populist imagination, whether religious or environmentalist, has always warmed to catastrophes, because the threat of them concentrates the mind so wonderfully. Global warming, if it is happening at all, is doing so with what to activists must seem maddening slowness. Recent results from the University of Alabama suggest that the average global temperature has now been cooling for 20 successive months, ever since soon after Mount Pinatubo erupted.

In any case, the greenhouse effect was last decade's threat. As a cause of anxiety, a collision with an asteroid seems to be much more in keeping with the last decade of a millennium. To celebrate its 150th anniversary, *The Economist* recently argued for preparing to dispose of nuclear weapons by firing them at any asteroid that dare come too close. There is an issue to torture the liberal conscience.

Perhaps the word 'maastricht' will come to have a general meaning for a *fin de siècle* calm before an Armageddon-like storm: from ante-diluvian to post-maastrichtian.

2.   Myths of Population Growth*

For ambitious environmentalists, the place to be seen this year will be Cairo, at the United Nations population jamboree in September. Population was the issue that got away at the Earth Summit at Rio de Janeiro two years ago: those naughty Catholics succeeded in keeping it off the agenda. This year's Cairo meeting will put that omission right. In the intervening months prepare to be inundated with propaganda about our disgraceful fecundity.

Thomas Malthus was right. The world cannot support an infinite number of people, so eventually, if population continues to increase, the number of people will start to grow faster than their food supply, and famine will be inevitable. The trouble with Malthus is that tricky word 'eventually'. The earnest clergyman was worried about Britain, a country in which 'eventually' never came because soon after he was writing, the demographic transition caused the birth rate to plummet even faster than the death rate, and the population stopped growing. The productivity of agriculture, meanwhile, has gone on increasing steadily.

'We shouldn't delude ourselves,' write Paul and Anne Ehrlich, the most famous of modern malthusiasts:

> 'The population explosion will come to an end before very long. The only remaining question is whether it will be halted through the humane method of birth control, or by nature wiping out the surplus.'[1]

Yet country after country is following Britain through the demographic transition. In almost no country is the rate of population increase accelerating. In countries like Thailand it is decelerating rapidly. Even the most alarmist projections expect the rate of increase of the world population to decelerate steadily until it levels off at zero, probably long before 2100 and probably well below 15 billion people.

So the only question we need worry about is whether the

---

*Published as 'Food for thought if birth rate of the world trebles' in *The Sunday Telegraph* on 22 May 1994.

[1] In Jonathan Porritt (ed.), *Save the Earth*, Channel 4 Books and Dorling Kindersley, 1991, p. 119.

planet can support 15 billion people. Conventional wisdom assumes not. Yet we have survived a fivefold increase since Malthus's time. Indeed, as Julian Simon, the malthusiasts' gadfly, has argued, we have not just survived: we have thrived.

Relative to wages, food prices have fallen to one-tenth their levels in 1800. Per-person food consumption is greater world-wide than ever before. Deaths from famine are at their lowest level ever, both in absolute numbers and relative to other deaths. Mass starvation still happens, but usually because of war, not agricultural failure. There is virtually no natural resource that is scarcer now than it was in 1800. There are more proven reserves of oil now than at any moment in the past. The price of copper was 100 times as high (in terms of wages) in the Roman empire as now.

If we have survived a fivefold increase in population, can we stand another trebling? Something, surely, will run out: if not food, then energy, or water, or the capacity of the atmosphere to absorb our pollution. Professor Simon argues not. Crises and shortages prove again and again to be nothing but spurs to invention. The fuel wood crisis of the 17th century led directly to the development of coal and water as sources of power. The whale oil crisis of the 1840s spurred ingenious men to search for petroleum. If oil were to run out soon, there are limitless technologies waiting for energy prices to rise sufficiently to make them viable: many of them – like solar and nuclear – ones that produce no carbon dioxide.

America's National Academy of Sciences changed its mind about population a few years ago and admitted: 'The scarcity of exhaustible resources is at most a minor restraint on economic growth.' Despite tremendous efforts to find one, nobody has yet proved that population growth causes poverty. Quite the reverse: countries with high population growths, and high population densities, generally enjoy faster economic growth than sparser, more demographically stagnant countries. Call me irresponsible if you like, but I am prepared to wager that the world will prove capable of supporting 15 billion people in 2100 at greater average prosperity than we enjoy today. Whether we want it to is a different matter.

3. The Thriving North Sea*

Every few years, the newspapers fill up with headlines about 'North Sea in danger'. Last month a meeting of environment ministers in Copenhagen was the excuse for leaking a draft report on the environmental problems of the North Sea, called the Quality Status Report or QSR, which is part of preparation for the North Sea conference of 1995. The quality of the North Sea, it emerges, is dire.

The authors of such a report concentrate, as they should, on the things that are wrong with the sea. The layman is therefore left with the impression that things are getting worse, an impression that the press only exacerbates. It rushes to quote somebody from, say, the World Wide Fund for Nature, who, intent on saying something newsworthy, 'calls' (as he should – he is a lobbyist) for something dramatic: in this case a nature reserve to cover 10 per cent of the sea.

The result is a terrifying picture of such a noxious chemical brew that dog whelks are changing sex, dabs are developing tumours, dolphins' livers are going wrong, and razorbills are dying out because of oil spills.

None of this is technically wrong. Reputable scientists have confirmed that tributyl TIN, the anti-fouling paint used on ships' bottoms, does have the bizarre consequence of making dog whelks change into bitch whelks (although, if I recall my undergraduate biology correctly, many molluscs change sex at some point in their lives anyway). The increase in tumours on dabs is genuine. The overfishing of certain fish is undeniable.

But there is a difference between spotting a problem, such as anti-fouling paint, and crying apocalypse. The North Sea is not dead, not dying, not even sick. How do I know this? Well, close to where I live there is a group of offshore islands called the Farne Islands, which constitute one of the most spectacular bird sanctuaries in the world, let alone the North Sea. Over 60,000 pairs of sea birds nest on these islands. The birds are at the end of a longish food chain, because they eat fish, which mostly eat

---

*Published as 'Devilish words do an injustice to our deep blue sea' in *The Sunday Telegraph* on 2 January 1994.

15

smaller fish, which eat things that eat plankton. They are therefore well placed to accumulate any poisons that are in the sea. They are less than 100 miles from the chemical complex of Teeside and the industrial complex of Tyneside. Seabird colonies like the Farnes are, as it were, the miners' canaries of the North Sea.

And they tell an unambiguous story. Since 1971 the number of nesting birds has more than doubled. The razorbill, which is singled out in the QSR as a victim of oil pollution, is rare on the Farnes, but it is not nearly as rare as it was. When I was young there were usually a few pairs of razorbills, and it took all afternoon to find one amongst the milling flocks of guillemots. Today there are more than 100 pairs. In 20 years guillemots have increased by 800 per cent; kittiwakes have doubled in number; shags are up tenfold; eider ducks have doubled; and puffins are now up to the incredible figure of nearly 30,000 nesting pairs. Only terns, which spend three-quarters of the year not in the North Sea at all, but on migration to the southern oceans, have failed to increase by more than a slight number.

I have taken friends to the Farnes and seen their minds boggled by the sight of deep, clear, blue water breaking on cliffs that are literally covered in thousands of birds, and in which a diving seal is visible for a long way down. The friends' minds were boggled because they had formed the impression that the North Sea is all grey-brown and poisoned. They had believed that all the seals died in the late-1980s because of pollution, when in truth there was never a shred of evidence to link the epidemic of distemper virus that killed some seals in those years with pollution, any more than the current human epidemic of Beijing flu can be blamed on pollution.

We need to develop a way of talking about pollution problems without the mendacious hyperbole. Yes, oil slicks have killed individual razorbills, but they have not threatened the species, which is thriving as never before. Yes, anti-fouling paint is a new pollution problem, and sewage is an old one, but other pollution problems have largely been solved. DDT is not building up in the North Sea; it is disappearing. And, as a summary of the QSR says (unreported in the newspapers), 'concentrations of contaminants only appear to reach levels where environmental impact might arise in areas close to likely sources, e.g. in estuaries'. In other words, marine pollution in the North Sea is a local problem, not a general one.

4. Asthma and Car Fumes*

Bashing the car seems to be the environmental sport of the moment. If ever something looked unsustainable, it is building ever more roads for ever more cars in an increasingly NIMBY-minded country. So I might as well add my own boot to the kicking. I have a feeling that we are on the brink of discovering that cars cause general (as opposed to occupational or accidental) ill-health, about the first time since lead pipes finished the Romans that we can make such a claim for any technology.

Although environmentalists would have you believe otherwise, we are steadily eliminating technology as a cause of premature death or ill-health in Western society. To be sure, people are still knocked down by buses and poisoned by weedkiller. But pollution has not, despite frequent attempts to claim the contrary, had any effects on cancer rates, which (corrected for age) are falling. Despite pesticides, fossil fuels, nuclear power, preservatives, dioxin, high-voltage wires, fluoride, acid rain, chlorofluorocarbons – despite all these things we live longer, healthier lives than ever before.

I say this not to be Panglossian, but because there is one enormous exception to the good news. Allergy – from asthma to hay fever – is a modern, Western, prosperous disease. It is virtually absent from literature and history until the present century; and even today it is almost unknown in the Third World. It is also worse in cities than in rural areas.

Unlike almost every other chronic disease, it is getting worse. Hospital admissions for childhood asthma have doubled since the 1970s. The proportion of boys aged six to 12 with asthma has risen from 2·4 per cent in 1980 to 3·6 per cent in 1990 (girls are less susceptible). Far more young people than old suffer from hay fever.

And yet the immediate causes of allergy are in decline. As a new booklet published last week explained, grass pollen, the main trigger of hay fever, is less abundant and around for fewer days a year than ever before, thanks to the disappearance of hay meadows under concrete, corn or trees.

---

*Published as 'Why cars can be seriously bad for your health' in *The Sunday Telegraph* on 13 February 1994.

Although asthma and hay fever are also 'caused' by genetics, in the sense that people inherit susceptibility from their parents (I seem to be lucky and have never had any allergy), something in modern urban life is triggering that susceptibility more than it once did. What?

It seems there are two leading explanations, each with very different implications. Allergies are caused by the misfiring of part of the immune system, known as the IgE network. Unlike the other parts of the immune system, the IgG and IgL, which defend the blood against bacteria and viruses, IgE is designed to attack foreign bodies on the 'outer' surfaces of the body: the skin, the gut and airways. Back in the Stone Age the IgE was fully employed fending off the attentions of worms, amoebae and other parasites: all the various creatures that try to make a home in human lungs, guts and skin.

So the first theory is that we have simply become too hygienic. The IgE network, bored and frustrated by the lack of challenges in life, simply turns on an unsuspecting piece of grass pollen as if it were a tapeworm and mounts a full-scale assault to get rid of it. The answer to hay fever may therefore be the judicious exposure of your children to a menagerie of parasitic worms.

There is some direct evidence for this idea, but not much. It seems more likely that car exhaust is responsible. After all, living next to a busy road can trigger an asthma attack in an asthmatic, so it seems logical that it can trigger asthma in a non-asthmatic. Car fumes are about the only air pollutants that have been increasing steadily in recent decades. The National Asthma Campaign, while striving to add caveats, is virtually certain that nitrogen oxides are the main culprits.

This is one environmental scare that I find convincing. But not until they had invented a strain of rabbit that gets asthma were scientists able to test this suggestion directly. I understand this is now the case and that in a laboratory in London there are now potentially asthmatic rabbits breathing fresh air next to rabbits breathing car fumes. The car industry should prepare for the results.

PART II

CLIMATE CHANGE

5.   Sulphur in the Greenhouse*

It may not seem like it to a VAT-threatened pensioner, but the nights are getting warmer. In all the noise and fury of the global warming debate, where no statistic is beyond challenge, or ever proves any theory true beyond doubt, there is one fact that has become uncontroversial. The difference between night-time temperatures and day-time temperatures is shrinking all over the world. The best explanation of this fact is an uncomfortable one: one kind of pollution is keeping us warm at night, and another is keeping us cool by day. If we stop producing one, but not the other, there will be trouble.

At thousands of places throughout the world, ranging from the Aleutians to the Outback, diligent unsung heroes collect daily maximum and minimum temperatures and send them in to some all-knowing computer. In 90 per cent of these places, the average difference between maximum and minimum is shrinking steadily. In 10 per cent it is growing. This is not because the unsung heroes live in cities (which are warmer both in the day and at night), because those who live in remote spots have recorded just as great a fall in the daily temperature range. On the top of the Pic du Midi, in the Pyrenees, the warmer nights have been especially noticeable.

In America and Russia the records are good enough to suggest that this is a recent trend, which began in the 1950s. Before that there was no tendency for the daily temperature range to shrink. Since then, however, daily minimum temperatures from all over the world have risen three times as fast as daily maxima, which have hardly budged at all – and in some cases have shrunk. Or, to put it another way, global warming is happening almost exclusively at night.

The explanation seems to be that skies are getting cloudier. Clouds keep the daytime temperature down by reflecting sunlight back into space, and they keep the night warmer by trapping the day's warmth. It is one of my favourite miscellaneous facts that in the Eocene period, 40 million years ago,

---

*Published as 'Sulphur does not really deserve its brimstone image' in *The Sunday Telegraph* on 28 November 1993.

frost was rare at the North Pole, probably because cloud cover over the Arctic was total and continuous, thanks to too much methane in the atmosphere. Trees grew on northern Greenland.

But why are clouds increasing? This is where my climatologist acquaintances start to acquire a glint in their eyes. Sulphur dioxide, the gas that spews from the chimneys of coal-fired power stations and to a lesser extent from car engines and every other combustion engine, is an especially efficient cloudmaker chemical. Before 1950, most smokestacks were short, and more people burned coal in their grates, rather than buying electricity from coal burned in a distant power station's grate, so sulphur dioxide did not stay in the air for long or travel far. It came down and poisoned lichens on nearby trees. Since the 1950s, we have spewed the stuff into the upper atmosphere, where it seeds the clouds. The contrails of high-flying jets are another source of new cloudiness in the upper atmosphere.

More clouds mean less heat loss at night, but less heat gain in the daytime. Hence the puzzling failure of average temperatures to rise as fast as predicted by greenhouse-effect fans. Sulphur dioxide emissions are keeping them down in the daytime.

This raises the intriguing possibility that the expensive measures we have been dragooned into taking against acid rain will, by cutting sulphur emissions, actually deliver us into the global warming frying pan. Global warming will no longer be confined to the night by a nice protective shield of sulphur-created clouds. What makes it all the more ironic is that the evidence on which we blamed sulphuric acid for the deaths of trees in Canada and Germany has proved to be almost entirely faulty. Sulphur dioxide has now been almost entirely exonerated from killing trees (though it did play a part in acidifying lakes). Too late to stop the juggernaut of international legislation forcing power stations to add expensive scrubbers.

I have often wondered how different the acid-rain debate would have been if sulphur (brimstone) had not been culturally associated with evil. From the early days of the debate, some of us were pointing out that the evidence pointed at nitrogen oxides, not sulphur, but nobody paid much attention. Despite being a vital ingredient in explosives, nitrogen has always been one of chemistry's good guys. Sulphur has always been a villain.

6. Doubts About the Warming*

The timing was delicious. In the week that scientists announced strong evidence that the planet's temperature has not increased at all between 1979 and 1993, the Government announced its plans for dealing with that increase.

The scientists in question, from the University of Alabama, have taken the globe's temperature by satellite and their results are in this week's *Nature*. Until now global temperature was estimated by compiling ground-based records from all over the world and averaging them. This produces a fairly unambiguous picture: no change between 1860 and 1910, a steady increase of 0·4 of a degree between 1910 and 1940, no change between 1940 and 1980, and a steady increase of 0·3 of a degree between 1980 and 1990. It is this set of data that underlies all of the greenhouse debate, including the Government's own 'action plan', announced this week.

The satellites, however, tell a very different story about the 1980s (their data do not go farther back). Orbiting from north to south as the Earth turns beneath them, they take the temperature of the lower atmosphere using microwave sensors. By the end of 1993 the temperature was trending *downwards* by 0·04 of a degree per decade.

The satellite's masters explain away this awkward fact by subtracting two volcanic eruptions (Mount Pinatubo in 1991 and El Chichon in 1982) and four El Ninos (sudden changes in the circulation of the water in the Pacific). Since they assume that all these would have cooled the atmosphere, they conclude that the 1980s did see a gradual warming of the air by 0·09 degrees: still less than a third of that recorded by the old method.

Even with this sleight of hand (and when I was a scientist I was trained not to correct my data according to my preconceptions of the result), the startling truth remains that the best measure yet taken of the atmosphere has found virtually no evidence of global warming. After the hullabaloo of recent years, you would think this might rate a mention in the media. Not a peep.

---

*Published as 'Scientists pour cold water on global warming' in *The Sunday Telegraph* on 30 January 1994.

My environmentalist friends will respond by arguing that the theory still seems to suggest that all our emissions of carbon dioxide *should* be trapping the sun's reflected heat and that their worries are based not on the evidence that they *are* doing so but on the prediction that they *might* do so. This is known as the precautionary principle: better safe than sorry. The Government explicitly said this week that it bases its whole plan on this caution:

> '[I]t is appropriate to take action ahead of unequivocal evidence being established about the nature and possible effects of man-made climate change.'

Global warming, in other words, must be treated as guilty until proven innocent, because the cost of presuming innocence and being wrong might be greater than the cost of presuming guilt and being wrong. This is a reversal of the usual scientific rules under which a new theory is treated as suspect until some evidence is produced for it.

I used to think this suspension of the rules for global warming was right, but I am increasingly unsure. Not only has the theory repeatedly failed empirical tests, but it has also begun to fall apart as a theory. It now seems that the wavelength of radiation that carbon dioxide absorbs may be already saturated: that is, the existing carbon dioxide absorbs it all, so extra carbon dioxide will absorb no more. Moreover, the precautionary principle could prove to be economically wrong as well. The cost of doing something now might be more expensive than the cost of adjusting to a degree or two of warming in a century.

The boot should be on the other foot: global warming must lose its special status as a theory assumed right until proven wrong. It is a normal hypothesis, one for which the evidence is now, after intensive research, less convincing than it was before. It may be far too late for such common sense to prevail. Government bureaucracy and public opinion now both assume that global warming is a proven fact. Changing the latter may be possible, but the former, like a time-travelling supertanker, takes decades to change its mind.

7. Greenpeace's Propaganda*

The more I write about global warming, the more doubts I have about it. Not because the facts change, but because the theory's defenders put up such weak arguments when you raise doubts. The last time I touched on the issue, I was treated to a letter of vertiginous condescension by Sir John Houghton, one of the chairmen of the Intergovernmental Panel on Climate Change. Pity oozed from his every phrase, yet there was not a single fact in his letter that contradicted the doubts I had raised. Indeed, in his last sentence, he even made the same point I had made – that there has never yet been a century without several degrees of climate change – without apparently realising that I had drawn the opposite conclusion from it.

I still think future global warming caused by man-made carbon dioxide is a strong possibility. But the alarmists are growing so fantastical in their claims and so complacent in their certainty that we will all believe anything they say, that they are becoming their own worst enemies.

Take this month's offering from Greenpeace, which has just published what it calls an 'international climate database', which 'catalogues the growth of observable climate change phenomena' by 'drawing on published sources, scientific and technical studies'. This all sounds, as it is supposed to, very professional and useful. So I turned to it hopefully. It is a list of newspaper cuttings (I suppose that is what 'drawing on published sources' means), very few of which concern facts, and almost all of which merely report speculation by Greenpeace-like alarmists. If this is a database, *The Sun* is an encyclopaedia.

Here are some of the 'facts' Greenpeace highlights (my italics): 'The intensity and severity of storms *is likely to* increase'; 'Lloyd's of London is facing ruin'; 'global warming *would* reduce global food production'; 'the best *forecast* for sea-level rise is 3-10 millimetres a year'; 'an explosion of moths, beetles and spiders *could* wreak havoc on crops, forests and human health'; 'malaria, asthma, encephalitis, leprosy, dengue fever and measles are all

---

*Published as 'More hot air than facts on global warming' in *The Sunday Telegraph* on 26 June 1994.

expected to become more common'. Even if these predictions prove true, most have no demonstrable link with global warming. Those that do presuppose the very trend they are supposed to support.

Most climate scientists are careful to deny that short-term fluctuations in weather have anything to do with long-term climate change. Greenpeace has no such qualms. It cites last winter's floods in France and New Zealand, some recent hurricanes, California's bush fires, and all sorts of other random natural disasters as evidence for global climate change. Oddly, it omits America's record cold winter last year, which *Time* magazine said heralded the next ice age.

Even Greenpeace's favourite fact – the eight hottest years on record have occurred since 1980 – is badly out of date. New satellite data reveal no increasing trend at all, while correcting for the fact that many ground-based weather stations are in urbanising or desertifying areas makes the 1980s normal, not exceptional. If this Greenpeace document represents the best that defenders of climate-change theory can do, then the doubters have a point.

If I were to write this about a typical vested interest – the Government, say, or the tobacco lobby – it would neither surprise nor shock people. Of course, vested interests fib and exaggerate and select their facts to make their case. The puzzle is not why green lobbyists also do this. They are operating in a competitive market for people's contributions and he who lags behind soon loses revenue. The surprise is why people consistently fail to take green pronouncements with a pinch of salt.

Environmentalists have realised in the past few years that they can get away with murder. People will believe anything and everything they say. In a recent poll by MORI, 73 per cent of people said they would trust a scientist working for an environmental organisation, whereas only 38 per cent would believe one working for the Government. Greenpeace and its ally-competitors are simply abusing that trust.

26

8. Ozone Exaggeration*

We are now to be warned by television weather forecasters when there is a danger of sunburn. I thought that most people knew that this occurred during sunshine, but the Health Education Authority, which endorsed the new idea, clearly knows better. Perhaps soon, rather than tell us it is going to rain, they will also remind us that we might therefore get wet.

The official campaign of terror about sunlight is gathering speed. Last summer, I read an interview with the Australian cricketer, Shane Warne, who greeted our cloudy skies decked out like an Apache and warned 'you Poms had better get wised up about skin cancer'. A radio report from Australia the other day had a British emigrant praising her new country for the way its government kept its citizens scared about the new dangers of skin cancer since the depletion of the ozone layer began. (For her and Mr Warne's information, northern Australia receives three times as much ultra-violet radiation as Britain, so even if they are right to be scared, the same may not apply to us.)

Unfortunately for the alarmists, the facts are awkward. Ultra-violet light does cause skin cancer in fair-skinned people, but of two relatively harmless types: basal cell carcinoma and squamous cell carcinoma. Both are very easily cured; fewer than 1 per cent of sufferers die from them. There is as yet no good evidence that links the much rarer and more lethal cancer known as malignant melanoma with sunlight. Malignant melanoma is a cancer that starts with a mole and usually occurs first on a part of the skin that is *not* exposed to the sun: the buttock is typical. It is also, in Australia, more common in people who work indoors than in people who work in the open air. This fits with the theory that it is the sudden exposure of very white skin – sunburn – rather than gradual exposure – suntan – that does worse damage. But who was in favour of sunburn anyway?

Besides, some exposure to ultra-violet rays is good for you, which is why Europeans developed fair skin in the first place. Without it, several diseases including rickets, osteomalacia

---

*Published as 'Taking the sting out of the great sunshine myth' in *The Sunday Telegraph* on 3 April 1994.

(brittle bones) and perhaps breast cancer are more common. Through such diseases more people may be dying from too little exposure to sunlight than too much.

Then comes the claim that ultra-violet light is increasing because of the thinning of the ozone shield. I used to believe this until I examined the evidence closely. What thinning of the ozone shield? The amount of ultra-violet-B radiation reaching the Earth is *decreasing* at the rate of 0·7 per cent a year largely because the amount of ozone in the atmosphere is *increasing*. True, there is a seasonal ozone 'hole' – in which the ozone concentration drops to half its usual level – over Antarctica, but even that could still be a natural phenomenon. It has occurred ever since scientists looked for it in 1957. And who ever sunbathed in Antarctica in late winter?

Reports of a northern ozone hole, by the way, were fabrications. Some over-excited scientists, keen to win new grants, over-interpreted data showing that some ozone-eating chemicals were present in the northern hemisphere. Reports of cataract-afflicted sheep in Chile were true, but irrelevant: they had caught an infectious disease.

The official prediction from America's National Academy of Sciences is, none the less, that the ozone layer over your head will be depleted by 5 per cent during the next century, which would expose you to more ultra-violet rays than you already receive. How much more? It would be equivalent to moving south by 30 miles. So if you think you could move south by a third of a mile a year and know how to cope with the extra risk of sunburn, then relax about the ozone layer.

As for covering ourselves in sun cream and wearing floppy hats, consider this. When you eventually take the hat off, you may be taking a greater risk *because* you covered up before. Melanoma, remember, has no link with suntan but a possible link with sunburn. So nobody – be he weather forecaster, health official or bossy neighbour – has any scientific right to lecture us on sunlight. Remember it was health officials in the 1970s that told us to put babies to sleep on their stomachs, and so caused an unnecessary increase in cot deaths.

PART III

THE COUNTRYSIDE

9. Hedges and Birds*

A £3 million government study of the countryside released this week has proved what we all knew: that modern farming is gradually impoverishing the natural history of farmland. It is getting better and better at making sure that all the sun's energy ends up in crops, so less and less ends up in pretty flowers and birds. But like so many such studies, it has led everybody to jump to the wrong conclusions. In particular, the usual tendency of conservationists to want to protect strongholds, rather than improve weakholds, was much in evidence this week.

Take the issue of hedges (or 'hedgerows', as I must learn to call them). Many lobbyists used this report as a cue to argue that legal protection for remaining hedges is needed. This is shutting the stable door after the horse has bolted. Those farmers who have not yet ripped out their hedges are mostly the ones with green tendencies. To slap them with an intrusive new legal obligation, expensively policed by bureaucrats, while letting their more anti-hedge brethren off free is to punish the innocent. Likewise, to bribe farmers to replace hedges they have already removed, as the Countryside Commission does, is to reward the guilty.

A better solution would be to adjust agricultural subsidies according to the average size of field on a farm. It would require about three lines of computer code in the Ministry of Agriculture's computer. At vast inconvenience and expense, farmers were made to fill out horrendously complicated forms earlier this year listing each field and describing its boundaries, so the data are there. Suppose farmers got a bonus of £10 an acre if all their fields averaged 15 acres or fewer, or a fine of £10 an acre if they averaged more than 50 acres. On a 300-acre farm the difference would be £6,000: less than the cost of planting a few hedges. Oh, I know, sorry. Brussels would not let us. Silly me.

But hedges are not the main problem in any case. It is what is happening in the open field that is more worrying. The British Trust for Ornithology last month estimated that we have lost

---

*Published as 'Don't bet your hedges to save the countryside' in *The Sunday Telegraph* on 21 November 1993.

31

more than three million skylarks from farmland since the 1970s, a more massive population collapse than for any other species, and a terrible loss of blithe-spirited song from spring. Skylarks do not go near hedges, so the blame must lie, say conservationists, with pesticides. Yet, where I live, there has been a marked decline in skylark numbers despite decreasing use of pesticides. I suspect a far more obvious cause is staring us in the face: the switch to winter-sown corn.

In the 1970s, after harvest, many wheat stubbles were still left over the winter to be sown with spring barley after April. New varieties of winter barley, and the introduction of oil-seed rape as a break crop between wheats, have altered that forever in most of lowland Britain. Spring barley was 25 per cent of the crop as late as 1982; it is virtually unknown in lowland England now. Now the plough and the drill follow days or even hours behind the combine harvester, preparing next year's crop. So all the wheat seeds and weed seeds that were on the stubble get buried and become food for bacteria and slugs instead of birds.

It occurs to me that if I were dictator, I could save the EC budget and the skylark with one decree. I would ban the cultivation of land between July 1st and March 1st. That would ensure an ample supply of stubble fields for birds through the winter and reduce cereal and rape yields by more than enough to cause the current surpluses to evaporate. It would also, however, drive most farmers bankrupt.

I leave you with a challenge. Although many of the larks, finches, buntings and sparrows that use open farmland have declined since the 1970s, some of them precipitously, one species stands out. It is a bird of hedges and arable farmland, which feeds on winter stubbles in large flocks. In the 1970s it was the commonest farmland bird. Every hedge that disappeared removed its nesting habitat; every spray of pesticide killed insects on which it fed its chicks; every autumn plough buried the seeds that would have seen it through the winter. Yet it is commoner than ever. On farmland, it now outnumbers all other finches, buntings and larks put together. And its numbers have grown by more than half a million on the BTO's census plots in 15 years. What is the chaffinch's secret?

10. Set-aside Folly*

As silly ideas for wasting public money go, paying farmers not to farm is high on the list. This is a truth universally acknowledged among environmentalists, the Ramblers' Association being the latest group to join in the successful bloodsport of 'set-aside'-bashing. But like most other groups on this particular bandwagon, the ramblers took the opportunity to miss the point.

Not that I would defend a policy of paying farmers to set arable land aside. All farm subsidies are a conspiracy of producers to defraud consumers and the money mostly ends up in the hands of property speculators, machinery manufacturers and chemical companies rather than farmers in any case. But I have yet to meet an environmentalist who wants these subsidies reduced. What they want is for them to be redirected into environmental projects.

The Ramblers, for example, contrast the figure of £853 million that will be paid in arable subsidy payments with the comparatively derisory £43 million that will be paid to farmers for environmental schemes. They call for more to be spent on the latter. Would it not be cheaper to stop paying the £853 million in the first place?

New Zealand stopped subsidising its farmers 10 years ago. Not only have most of them thrived, but the effect on the environment, according to a recent report, has been wholly beneficial. There is little doubt that, if we stopped subsidising farming in Britain, fewer pesticides and fertilisers would be used as farmers tried to cut costs; and some marginal land would come out of production to become a refuge for nature. Saving £853 million and the environment at the same time would be attractive to most environmentalists, you would think.

But it is not. Why? Because most environmental organisations need a good flow of public grants, contracts and consulting fees to keep them in business. Thus the game of demanding a subsidy to counteract the effect of other subsidies comes

---

*Published as 'Set greed aside to save millions and our wildlife' in *The Sunday Telegraph* on 5 December 1993.

naturally to them. There is nothing malicious or even conscious in this; it is just the way the world works.

So they miss the fact that it is up to them now to make set-aside an environmental project. Most farmers, given that they cannot grow crops on 15 per cent of their land (that is, if they choose the option of 'rotational' set-aside in which a field is set-aside for one year at a time), are glad to be told how to make it produce wildlife instead. Yet they are getting virtually no such advice. This is the second year of set-aside, but I have heard of only one environmental organisation that is actively seeking out farmers to tell them what they can do to help wildlife. The others are happier screaming for more public spending.

That organisation is the Game Conservancy, which has been trying hard to get the rules made friendly for partridges and to advise farmers what to do. Last year most farmers did what the ministry told them to do, which was nothing until May 1st and then cut the weeds before they set seed. The result was that a lovely, weedy mess grew up all over empty stubble fields, attracting all sorts of birds to nest and feed in it, whereupon the haymower came along in mid-breeding season like a Mongol horde and wiped out all the nests. Some farmers even found themselves chewing up roe deer fawns.

One alternative is to plough the fields in March. This provides the bare land that birds such as peewits like to nest on. Indeed, the Royal Society for the Protection of Birds leans towards suggesting this because it is at least less bad than ploughing or cutting in May or June.

But the Game Conservancy is exercised about sawflies, insects that spend the winter in the soil and the summer in the corn, where they provide the staple diet of partridge chicks, skylarks and so forth. Ploughing before May 10th kills most of the sawflies in the soil. Yet by May 10th, the field is full of birds' nests. And by May 25th the most tiresome weedy grasses such as barren brome are already setting seed.

So, ironically, given that farmers will insist on doing something to control the weeds that would otherwise infest next year's crop, the most environmentally friendly option is probably to spray the field with herbicide in mid-May. The sprayer does not destroy nearly as many nests as the mower or plough, and the sawflies are by then safely gone abroad in search of corn. If the Ramblers and others disagree, what do they advise instead?

11. Butterflies and the Modern World*

In a letter in Tuesday's *Daily Telegraph*, Jilly Shaul complained about the disappearance of butterflies from her garden, wondered if new insecticides were the reason and asked for reassurance. Coincidentally, that same day I found an article in the Royal Forestry Society's journal that Mrs Shaul would have found far from reassuring. It detailed rapid recent declines in most woodland butterflies. Some, especially the various fritillaries, have declined by over 90 per cent in 30 years.

I called one of the authors of the article, Gary Roberts of 'Butterfly Conservation', who confirmed that the problem is not confined to woodland butterflies. Grassland species are in equally deep trouble. So if you think you are seeing fewer meadow browns and chalkhill blues than you did in your youth, it is not because you are a nostalgic old fibster. With a few exceptions, butterflies are growing scarcer.

The main culprit is not pollution, not even pesticides (which are not often used in woods or meadows), but habitat changes. In woodland, this means especially the end of coppicing; and in grassland, it means the disappearance of downland under the plough. If there is a common theme it is intensification: the planting of dense crops of trees for timber production, rather than the harvesting of coppiced faggots from natural woodland; and the sowing and reaping of wheat where once there was pasture and meadow.

This explanation is supported by the exceptions that prove the rule. Some butterflies, such as the white admiral, are bucking the trend and expanding their range. White admirals prefer dense, shady woods, where their caterpillars can feed on honeysuckle. They welcome modern plantations. But the majority prefer the mosaic of habitats created by traditional coppicing: clearings, open glades, dense stands and mature trees. Likewise, what chalk downland provided was not one perfect butterfly habitat but many different types of terrain: hot, almost bare turf where silver-spotted skippers could

*Published as 'Butterflies fall victim to man's interfering hand' in *The Sunday Telegraph* on 17 July 1994.

breed, lush grass for marbled whites and buckthorn scrub for brimstones.

The irony is that coppiced woodland and chalk downland are two artificial, man-made habitats. Just as many of our favourite birds, from skylarks to peewits, must have been scarce in primeval, forested Britain, so many of our favourite butterflies would have occurred only on sea cliffs or in storm-blown clearings. It is now widely agreed among ecologists that when mankind first invaded these islands he increased biodiversity, he did not decrease it. He created a patchwork where before there was monotony.

So why are we now undoing the good we once did? The answer lies in two equally repellent words: myxomatosis and government. The decline in rabbits in the 1950s led to an explosion of scrub in grassland, on commons and in open forest clearings.

That was a passing phase, as we now know. But government did and still does even more damage than rabbits. For it was government that made it economic for farmers to rip up downland for wheat fields; it was government that bribed landowners to replace ancient woodlands with timber crops. Left to the private sector, these things would never have happened, because they would never have paid. True, ancient coppicing traditions would still have mostly died out, but the rush to plant spruce, or to plough up marginal land, would not have occurred at all without Forestry Commission tax breaks and arable price supports.

Butterfly Conservation, which runs some excellent butterfly reserves, has produced a booklet on woodland management for butterflies. It also wants landowners to get grants for coppicing and traditional management. I am against this. Giving government more of our money to undo damage it does with our money is like putting arsonists in charge of fire brigades: good for business, bad for wallets. Why not stop subsidising farming and forestry first?

12. The Decline of the Red Squirrel*

Tomorrow sees the launch of Red Alert North West, a campaign to defend one of the last strongholds of the red squirrel. The North-East has had such a campaign going for nearly two years. But we northerners, always quick to spot a southernist slight, are getting a little chippy about how little the south seems to appreciate the plight of red squirrels. They have been gone from the home counties for so long that the Quangos, Nogos and Gos that govern the conservation establishment seem to regard the battle to save them as lost. All official efforts to stem the spread of the grey squirrel ceased several decades ago.

There is a more potent reason for the lack of organised concern for the red squirrel. It is one of the very few environmental issues that starkly differentiates the goats of conservation from the sheep of animal welfare. For there is only one thing wrong with red squirrels in this country: grey squirrels. In May 1989, Silverdale in Cumbria had 16 resident red squirrels and no greys. Three years later, there were many resident greys and no reds.

The same has happened in wood after wood throughout England, Wales and lowland Scotland: as soon as greys arrive, reds die out. All the other excuses that have been tried over the years fail: habitat loss, disease, pollution. Red squirrels would be thriving all over the home counties if grey squirrels had not been introduced from America in 1876. The only way to stop the decline of red squirrels is to stop the spread of greys. But that is unfashionable because it places the blame not on the usual suspects, such as industrial polluters, or 'serried ranks of tax-break conifers' (red squirrels love them), but on other furry animals. Some environmentalists are curiously muted when they cannot blame capitalists.

Consider one of the most urgent measures that is needed. At present the law forbids anybody from poisoning grey squirrels in Durham, Cumbria or Northumberland, counties where reds still live. The reason is to prevent the killing of reds. Ironically, this

---

*Published as 'Tackle the grey area to save the red squirrel' in *The Sunday Telegraph* on 14 November 1993.

law could not be better designed to do harm to reds, because it means that nothing prevents the invading greys from building up to maximum density. Greys can live at six times the density of reds, and can eat things reds cannot, such as acorns, so the greys eat the reds' food supply. Arguably the free use of poison in the overlap zone would benefit the reds because greys are bolder about coming to feeding hoppers, and they would be held below the density where they drive out the reds.

In any case, thanks to experiments by Harry Pepper of the Forestry Commission, a hopper has now been designed that a grey can feed from but not a red. This can be filled with warfarin-tainted grain, a humane poison that is used for greys all over the rest of the country. A different kind of hopper that only reds can enter (they weigh half as much as greys) can be filled with untainted grain.

To animal lovers, poisoning grey squirrels is of course anathema, but responsible conservation has always posed hard choices. The red squirrel is an animal designed to survive in the pine and spruce forests of post-ice-age Europe, but because no other squirrels reached Europe, it adapted to broad-leaved forests as well. Now it is being driven out by a species honed by millennia for the task of surviving in oak forests, a species that left its parasites and natural enemies behind in North America and that, let us face it, is far less pretty to look at. There is no question where our duty as conservationists lies. It is to try to reverse the error of the introduction.

About five red squirrels come to my garden every morning. Each one takes peanuts from the bird table and buries them in the lawn, then finds and digs up the peanuts the others have buried and eats them. With their white shirt fronts, orange backs and tails and tufted ears, they are infinitely more appealing than greys. And they do no harm, except perhaps eating the odd bird's nest, whereas grey squirrels do terrible damage to woods and forests by gnawing at the bark of sapling trees. The cost to a forester of leaving grey squirrels unpoisoned can be up to £30 a hectare per year.

Once greys move in they can never be exterminated because their stronghold and reservoir is in parks and gardens in towns. Like magpies, they thrive so well in the cities that no amount of persecution in the countryside can do anything more than keep up with the flow from the cities. Once they establish themselves in a town, the surrounding country is lost to red squirrels forever.

13. Ethnic Cleansing and the Sycamore*

If you think political correctness and ethnic cleansing do not go together, you have never met a modern conservationist. Even as we celebrate becoming a multiracial society, environmentalists decry the presence of exotic and alien species in terms that would be positively racist if applied to human beings. Are they right to be so prejudiced against the foreign?

In some cases, yes. Undoubtedly, the introduction of exotic species has been a far greater cause of extinction than chemical pollution ever was. After Captain Cook had passed by, rats, cats and pigs wiped out many hundreds of island species in the Pacific. New Zealand settlers formed 'acclimatisation societies' to bring out birds and animals from Britain to make the settlers feel at home, which was catastrophic for the native birds of New Zealand. Various American species have wreaked havoc among our own native creatures (and vice versa): grey squirrels have all but exterminated red squirrels from southern England; mink are well on the way to wiping out water voles.

Yet eager bureaucrats are now becoming ridiculously over-zealous in their ethnic prejudice. A landowner acquaintance of mine in South Yorkshire applied to the Forestry Commission for permission (this is normal since the stealthy nationalisation of private forestry in the past decade) to underplant a mixed wood with young beech to replace senescent Capability Brown beech woods nearby. A young official visited him and vetoed the scheme. Reason? Beech is 'not native' to the Yorkshire limestone.

Quite apart from the effrontery of a government body – that until very recently urged and grant-aided the planting of little but sitka spruce (from Alaska) – now telling people not to plant beech, the young man's sensitivity is absurd. Ever since the ice age, the forests of Britain have been in a state of constant change as species shifted to adapt to the changing climate. Beech was one of the last species across the Dover land bridge and was still spreading north when history started. Must we fossilise one glimpse of this ever-changing view?

---

*Published as 'Ethnic cleansers who are barking up the wrong tree' in *The Sunday Telegraph* on 1 May 1994.

James Ogilvie, a more enlightened Forestry Commission conservator, points out to me that prejudice against the sycamore tree is the most bizarre. Among naturalists, the sycamore, an attractive and vigorous maple (though the name sycamore is used in America for plane trees), seems to be regarded by the environmental Gestapo as a desperate enemy, to be extirpated wherever it exists. The sycamore's crimes are that its vigorous seedlings invade some stands of ancient oak woodland, shading out the flowers on the forest floor, and that it supports many fewer insect species than oak trees. Both these faults are the result of its supposed foreignness: it was allegedly brought here by the Romans.

Yet, according to Morton Boyd, a former director of the Nature Conservancy Council in Scotland, most of this is nonsense. Sycamores are probably natural invaders, which have spread across Europe rather later than other trees and only reached Britain after the beginning of recorded history – of their own accord. Even if they did need man's help to get here, it was the historical accident of the English Channel that made it necessary, not some divine decree that Britain and sycamores were incompatible. Come to that, many oak trees in British woods are descended from French or German acorns brought here in recent centuries. Should they be rooted out, too?

As for the supposed ecological poverty of the sycamore, Mr Boyd gives it short shrift. A sycamore supports a greater weight of insects even than an oak, and provides more food for birds than beech, ash or hazel. Since the decline of the elm, sycamore supports more mosses and lichens than any other tree and almost as many toadstools as oak. Its leaf litter is the richest of any broadleaved tree, which is why worms (and hence woodcocks) like it so much.

Sycamore will invade under a thin oak canopy, true, but then oak invades under a thin sycamore canopy. So the spread of sycamore into ancient oak woodland is a natural part of the tree's historical arrival in these lands. There is nothing wrong with fighting it site by site to save wild flowers, but a general prejudice against the 'alien' sycamore is absurd.

PART IV

CONSERVATION

14. Exposing the Extinction Myths*

A letter to the magazine *Nature* this month brings into the open an argument that has been raging beneath the surface of biology: how many species are actually going extinct? The true answer – a worrying trickle – has for some time not satisfied ecologists, and they have been exaggerating madly to get attention. The whistle is now being blown on them.

'The imminent catastrophe in tropical forests is commensurate with all the great mass extinctions except for that at the end of the Permian.' 'Of the 3-10 million species now present on earth, at least 500,000 to 600,000 *will* be extinguished during the next two decades.' 'We face the prospect of losing 20 per cent of all species within 30 years and 50 per cent or more by the end of the next century.' 'Even with these cautious parameters, selected in a biased manner to draw a maximally optimistic conclusion, the number of species doomed each year is 27,000.'

These are statements from four highly respected scientists not on the payroll of environmental groups. They pale beside the remarks made by more radical Greens. Yet what is the actual evidence for them? There are about 13,000 known species of birds and mammals, and they have been dying out at the rate of just one species a year (that is, 0·00008 per cent) this century. Each one – the huia, the quagga, or the thylacine – is still a tragic loss, but at this rate it would take 2,600 years to wipe out 20 per cent of them, not 30 years.

Well, perhaps birds and mammals are not as badly off as other animals. Yet the evidence points the other way: large animals are more vulnerable to extinction than small ones. So perhaps the rate of extinction is about to expand rapidly. E. O. Wilson, author of the best-selling *The Diversity of Life*, uses this argument to justify his estimates of 50,000 species a year as 'committed to extinction' – that is, already as good as doomed.

But again the facts simply do not bear him out. Even if you stretch the definition, it is hard to identify more than 450 bird species that *will* be doomed by 2015 on current

---

*Published as 'Dying out, but not as fast as we thought' in *The Sunday Telegraph* on 31 July 1994.

trends, less than half the predicted number supposed to be unrescuable *now*.

The entire case for the large numbers is based on a theory, known as the species-area curve. This states that the number of species an island can support is strictly related to its size: an island 10 times the size of another will have twice as many species. Therefore, in theory, when you chop down 90 per cent of a kind of forest, half the species in it should die out.

Fortunately, they do not. The isolated Atlantic rain forests of south-east Brazil have been reduced to 12 per cent of their former extent. Yet not a single endemic bird that inhabits the forests has disappeared. Indeed, several species thought extinct have been recently rediscovered. For various reasons the species-area curve just does not work with forests.

This is the gist of Stephen Budiansky's letter to *Nature*, and he says that some biologists privately agree that he is right, but dare not say so for fear of rocking the boat. Budiansky, a naturalist and writer, has been subjected to torrential abuse from the biodiversity experts for wondering if their emperor is a bit nude.

The discrediting of the numbers will give comfort to the enemies of rain forests, undoubtedly, and succour to those who say nothing is wrong. So should people like Budiansky keep silent and let the end justify the means? Or should the fibs not have been told in the first place? The truth is bad enough: that a small trickle of wonderful species of animal and plant is being driven extinct by the destruction of the rain forest.

15. What Is Biodiversity?*

Of all the conventional wisdoms in the world, the following is surely impregnable: biodiversity is a good thing. Last year's Rio conference was dedicated to this proposition and our Government signed a piece of paper promising to preserve the stuff. So what exactly is biodiversity?

The short answer, to most people, is that biodiversity means neither more nor less than the tropical rain forest itself. In some ways this is not a bad approximation. A few years ago, a scientist named Alwyn Gentry spent a month climbing every single tree in a Trafalgar-square-sized patch of forest on the lower Rio Napu in Peru. The 606 trees on his patch proved to belong to 300 different species.

But such forests are not always so diverse. If Mr Gentry were to repeat his feat over one thousand times as many hectares in the *mbau* forests of north-east Zaire, he would find himself getting very bored. Nearly all the trees are of one species for hundreds of square miles: a species called *Gilbertiodendron*. This is *bona-fide* rain forest, all dark and dank and steamy, and it is surrounded by miles of more typical diverse forest. But it is remarkable for its biomonotony.

Mbau forests not only have few kinds of trees; they house few kinds of beetles and mushrooms and birds as well. They consist of one kind of tree that is very good at one thing: growing slowly and steadily, in the dark shade cast by its brethren, producing tough leaves that are hard to digest and take a long time to decay, and dropping heavy seeds that are too little nutritious to be carried away by animals. They are, ecologically speaking, ungenerous.

The point is that biomonotony is just as natural as biodiversity. In some ways, it is even more natural. There is growing evidence that if you disturb a biomonotonous rain forest, it is usually replaced by a biodiverse one, and that the biodiversity of most rain forests in fact reflects a history of disturbance by occasional epidemics, tornadoes, fires or even, in

---

*Published as 'Diverse views on diversity home in on habitat range' in *The Sunday Telegraph* on 31 October 1993.

the case of central America where the Maya people lived, human influences. You could argue that the cause of biodiversity is aided by logging in the *mbau* forests and others in Asia and Latin America that resemble them.

You do not need to travel to Zaire to find natural biomonotony. There is a great difference between the ecological generosity of, say, beech and oak. Oak trees do not cast a heavy shade but allow all sorts of plants to grow around their bases and support hundreds of kinds of insects. Beech trees create a bare desert beneath their dense shade and support a handful of kinds of insects. Choose any pair of trees you like and make the comparison: larch is one of the most generous trees of all; spruce is one of the least.

An even better example is bracken, the pestilential fern of open moorland. Just like the *mbau* forests, bracken spreads very slowly but creates a deep shade that no other plants can tolerate. So once it has arrived, it never retreats again. Almost nothing will eat bracken: not sheep, not birds, very few insects. It is like a centrally planned economy: there is not much in the shops and all competition is suppressed.

Nobody wants to see bracken extinct altogether, but equally nobody would argue that bracken moors are better for, say, birds than heather moors. Agriculture introduces a similar paradox into the biodiversity debate. On the one hand it is undeniable that without farming all sorts of species would become rare or vanish altogether: peewits, chickweed, harvest mice, partridges. Britain would be one endless, tedious oak forest. None the less, it is equally undeniable that farming means ecological simplification. It consists of diverting the sun's energy into a few species at the expense of others: wheat, cattle and cabbages, rather than trees, beetles and aphids.

If all the species in the world that did not live in the rain forest went extinct, the planet would have lost only about 10 per cent of its biodiversity. But the damage would surely be far greater than if 10 per cent of the species in the rain forest had vanished. In the latter case, the gaps in the rain forest would soon close, whereas in the former, we would have lost most mammals, mammals being bad at rain-forest life, and nothing would grow in Britain at all. It is diversity of habitats, not species, that really counts.

16. Exotic Species for the Farm*

On July 12th 1742, a shipwrecked naturalist named Georg Steller sat upon the shore of an island in the Bering Sea dissecting a large animal and fending off the Arctic foxes which kept stealing his inkstand. He was the only naturalist ever to see the animal alive, for within 30 years it was extinct, a victim of the attribute that could just as easily have been its saving grace: it was fatally tasty and tame, allowing Steller both to stroke its nose and to skewer it with a hook.

Steller's sea cow was probably the best candidate for domestication we have ever extinguished. It was a large, docile, seaweed-eating mammal, a ready-made marine cow. Its extinction is a forcible reminder of the economic, as well as aesthetic, possibilities we lose when we extinguish species, but it is also a salutary tale of the difficulties of domesticating new breeds.

In a month when the RSPCA grew exercised about the welfare of farmed ostriches, and the Natural Fibres Organisation urged farmers to plant nettles on their set-aside land, there seems to be increasing emphasis on finding exotic species to farm. The answer to all farmers' woes, it seems, is to grow something that Brussels bureaucrats have never heard of subsidising: wild boar, deer, llamas, cashmere goats, blueberries, flax, willow coppice, buckwheat.

This line of argument has long puzzled me, for the farming press is full of success stories from the world of exotic farming, yet the countryside remains populated monotonously with Friesian cattle, black-faced sheep, yellow rape and golden wheat. Even longhorn cattle and Tamworth pigs are disappearing.

The answer to this puzzle dawned on me the other day. The exotic farming industry is entirely based on the philosophy of pyramid selling. If you have ever received one of those irritatingly logical chain letters that urges you to send £10 to somebody further back up the chain, then send the letter on to five friends, you will see what I mean straight away. Such chain letters only work so long as they keep spreading. The moment

---

*Published as 'Sea-cow slaughter robbed us of marine dairies' in *The Sunday Telegraph* on 24 October 1993.

47

they start to falter, lots of people lose small amounts to pay for the large amount the person at the head of the chain receives.

In the same way, the fabulous profits of ostrich or llama farming are captured by the first people to enter the business because they can charge the earth selling breeding stock to the next people, who in turn are tempted into the industry by the thought of charging the same sums to the next buyers, and so on down the chain. All perfectly legal and above board, and all, up until a certain point, profitable. But then one day there are more stud ostriches or llamas or wild boars on the market than there are buyers for them. From then on, the price you can get is the true price the meat fetches at the butchers.

The lesson plainly is to start the next chain yourself. The trouble is, all the exotic domestic animals like llamas have already been tried, so it is now a matter of domesticating wild animals. Bison ranching is big business in the United States already, and bison ranches with attached restaurants are springing up in touristy parts of Germany, too. New Zealanders are moving on from red deer to tropical Asian deer called sambar. The Russians tried domesticating elk (moose) in the 1950s with some success. In Africa all sorts of antelope – kudu, impala, eland, oryx – are being ranched.

But the truth is that such wild animals never really take to farming. They retain too many wild instincts. True domestic animals have had thousands of generations of selection (deliberate and accidental) for the retention of infantile characteristics into adulthood: plumpness, tameness, a tendency to follow rather than lead. Most dogs are basically wolf puppies that never grow up; they have floppy ears, small teeth, short snouts and half-formed hunting behaviour such as retrieving (have you noticed how vicious dogs have longer snouts and more cocked ears than docile ones?).

That is why it is such a pity that two animals that came ready-made for domestication died out so long ago. The dodo would have made a delicious and easy pet: it was slow, flightless and put on weight rapidly (probably to get it through lean seasons). Unlike chickens, dodos might have enjoyed the battery life. Better still would have been Steller's sea cow. Imagine, if it had lived, the floating Steller's dairy farms in the sea lochs of Scotland, and their famous, smokey-rich, salty yoghurt. Yum.

17. Sustainable Use of Wildlife*

Largely unnoticed, a revolution has occurred in the world of African wildlife conservation. The long, post-war emphasis on national parks, game reserves and pure protection is ending in widespread disillusion. In its place, 'utilisation' is all the rage: the exploiting of animals, outside parks, in ways that contribute money to local people – through sport hunting, harvesting, specialist tourism and the like.

Nothing symbolises this better than the recent replacement of Richard Leakey as director of the Kenya Wildlife Service by David Western. Leakey harnessed his fame to a last, brave and abortive attempt to save the protectionist ideal. He raised funds abroad, gained control of his own budget and improved the esteem, weaponry and pay of park guards. Any gains now look unsustainable. Only eight of Kenya's 26 national parks are financially self-sufficient. His successor admits that the cost of continuing such policies to protect animals all across the country would be overwhelming. The emphasis has switched to encouraging game in the 93 per cent of the country that is not in national parks, by allowing judicious exploitation of animals by local people so that they have a stake in continued existence of the game.

Parks will survive, no doubt, but they will be increasingly degraded by the pressure of animals in them that no longer migrate, by poaching, cattle and by tourists themselves. The future for African wildlife must lie outside the parks as well.

If pure protection failed in Kenya, the most tourist-rich country, it is unlikely to succeed elsewhere. Indeed, southern Africa, especially Zimbabwe and Zambia, has long recognised the need to allow sustainable exploitation of wild animals outside parks if the indigenous people are to co-exist with wildlife. Zimbabwe's CAMPFIRE project, an innovative scheme to allow local people to profit from hunting and game farming, pioneered the new approach in the 1980s. Indeed, the success of such projects was the reason that southern African countries bitterly opposed the ivory trade ban a few years ago.

---

*Published as 'Why hunting makes a killing for game parks' in *The Sunday Telegraph* on 11 September 1994.

An influential book, Ray Bonner's *At the Hand of Man*, made this point forcibly last year, and excoriated the élitism of those who originally established the ideal of people-free reserves. The idea that a chunk of bush is somehow more 'natural' if it has had all the native inhabitants expelled from it is a cruel Western invention. Man has been a part of the African eco-system ever since he evolved from australopithecine apes three million years ago.

It would be nice to think that the way for Africans to exploit their local game would be to play host to groups of animal-lovers on safari on horse or foot, who wanted just to take pictures. In the long run, this may happen, but in the short run, most such peaceable tourists are still going to flock to the obvious honey-pots such as the Mara and the Kruger. For many years to come, the best source of income for a village in a dull, but buffalo-infested, part of the bush will be either to harvest hides and meat or to sell expensive licences to whites to hunt the animals. Hunters, unlike other tourists, spread out all across the country (to get away from each other and find untapped sources of trophies); and, unlike tourists, they pay steep prices. The Kenyan cabinet is already considering lifting its ban on sport hunting.

This places Western conservationists on the horns of a dilemma. Many of them recognise the justice of the case for sustained exploitation, but they depend for their funds on animal lovers in rich countries, who are usually moved to open their wallets by campaigns that appeal to animal welfare, rather than conservation itself. Will the World Wide Fund for Nature have the honesty to admit that killing elephants and buffalo for money can be crucial to conserving them?

18. The Ivory Ban Is Bad for Elephants*

Next week's meeting of the United Nation's Convention on International Trade in Endangered Species (CITES) in Florida will be, I confidently predict, the second-worst thing ever to happen to African elephants, the worst being the meeting of the same body five years ago, when ivory trading was banned. For the true enemies of elephants are the lobbyists arguing for the ban.

If you are inclined to condemn me as bonkers for taking such a line, I urge you to read a new booklet written by two curiously named Americans, Ike Sugg and Urs Kreuter, called *Elephants and Ivory*, and published by the Institute of Economic Affairs in London.

The booklet explodes many myths, the first and greatest being that the trade ban has 'worked'. The true price of traded ivory probably did fall steeply after the ban, though it is now rising again. There is good evidence that poaching of elephants decreased in some countries, notably Kenya, after the ban (and increased in others), but only where unsustainable amounts of Western money were suddenly poured into protection. In Zambia, poaching has increased except in the Luangwa valley where more money has been spent. In any case, poaching increased everywhere in 1993 as did the volume of ivory traded. The ban has not 'worked'.

So what has it achieved? To the extent that it devalued the ivory of legally killed elephants, it devalued elephants, and the only hope for their preservation is (a) to increase elephants' value and (b) ensure that such value can be captured by those who can control the elephants' fate – the local people.

Elephants are cuddly – to us. Not to most Africans, who suffer their depredations. 'The African farmer's enmity towards elephants is as visceral as Western mawkishness is passionate,' says the new head of the Kenya Wildlife Service. Add to this the fact that a Kenyan farmer cannot profit from an elephant and it is clear they are liabilities, not assets, to him. Reducing their value

---

*Published as 'UN's protection racket hurts the elephants' in *The Sunday Telegraph* on 6 November 1994.

51

even further is crazy. In Zimbabwe, the trading ban has cut revenue by $4 million, much of which was previously raised by small local communities that make a better living from auctioning hunting rights of carefully nurtured wildlife than they ever could from agriculture.

The ivory trade never has been the main threat to elephants. The threat was and is competition with farmers for land. Ivory merely gave people a reason to kill elephants in national parks as well as outside them.

Elephants would have been safe had not governments all over the continent nationalised them, thus removing from local people all chance to benefit from them and so all incentive to save them. Two statistics tell the story. Kenya banned hunting in 1976. Since then it has lost 85 per cent of its elephants. Zimbabwe granted landowners title to their wildlife in 1975; land devoted to wildlife increased from 17,000 to 30,000 square kilometres.

Sugg and Kreuter argue that 'preservation', which seeks to diminish the value of elephants and rely on negative incentives, will never be as effective as 'conservation', which seeks to increase and then devolve the benefits to be derived from wildlife. The elephant has value as a target for Western sportsmen, as a bearer of ivory, as a source of meat and hides, and – in most places only a distant last hope – as an attraction to tourists.

'If there is one thing we have learned in Africa it is that we cannot afford to be passionate about elephants and callous about people.' If there is one hope for elephants it is that the man who wrote those words, David Western, is now in charge of the Kenya Wildlife Service.

PART V

GREENS

19. The Central Planners of Rural England*

Last week's report from the Council for the Preservation of Rural England on leisure and the countryside promised to address the question of how we let people enjoy themselves in the country without spoiling others' fun. It is a good question, and I hoped to be shaken by it from my complacent view that it had an easy answer. I was disappointed.

My easy answer is that we do not allow things that spoil others' fun. As some philosopher once said, my right to swing my fist stops at your nose. Likewise, my right to enjoy myself recreating in the countryside stops when it interferes with your recreation. In theory this is a mightily difficult issue, because there are endless borderline cases. Does driving a caravan along a narrow road spoil the fun of the man behind who wants to drive fast to show off to his girlfriend or vice versa? And so on.

But, in practice, there is no need to get bogged down in grey areas. For example, if I were a dictator, using just three principles I reckon I could solve most problems fairly. First, a quiet activity would win over anything that makes a noise. So down with cross-country motorbikes, microlight aircraft, clay pigeon shoots and stereos. Second, highly visible recreation should always lose out to discreet pastimes. Thus, bird watchers and fishermen should win planning battles against balloonists and canoeists. Third, localised, 'honeypot' recreation is better for the country-side than activities that require large amounts of public space. So Center Parcs holiday villages tucked away in Longleat's woods seem a good idea, whereas Windermere water skiing entertains fewer people and spoils more people's fun.

However, I am not a dictator, so I turned to the CPRE report to find out how it thinks such matters should be settled. It had the clarifying effect of a smoke bomb in a fog. It was 72 pages of mind-bogglingly meaningless generalisations clothed in the jargon of the sociologist. It described disagreements as 'complex cultural tensions'; instead of more cars, it told of 'escalating private motorised mobility'. In trying to make the obvious point

---

*Published as 'Save us from the Central Planners of Rural England' in *The Sunday Telegraph* on 15 May 1994.

that some people care more about their hobbies than their jobs, it says:

> 'Such activities and affiliations may now frequently be playing an existentially more significant role, in that they help constitute the very identity of the individuals in question, in the contemporary cultural context that we have described.'

This is the language you would expect if you crossed Claude Levi-Strauss with Mr Pooter. Frankly, the CPRE has been diddled; the 'study' it commissioned, entirely lacking in specifics or even case studies, is distilled waffle. But it does have one dimly discernible message, a rather spooky one. Again and again the report criticises the fact that nobody is debating or 'acknowledging' the conflict between different leisure uses of the countryside. 'It is not too much to suggest,' intone the authors, 'that an unacknowledged cultural crisis is now crystallising around leisure and tourism trends in Britain.'

Mixed metaphors aside, where have these people been in the last few years, Mars? There is nothing unacknowledged about the impending public inquiry at Windermere on power boats; or about the disputes between foxhunters and saboteurs; the recent accommodation between white-water rafters and fishermen on the River Tay 'acknowledged' a problem and solved it. Then it suddenly dawned on me what the CPRE meant by unacknowledged. It meant uncentralised.

The whole report is suffused with the *dirigiste* itch of the central planner. It bemoans the 'continuing lack of new strategic thought' and says that local disputes should be treated as 'multi-faceted cultural tensions of truly national significance'; again and again it acts as if the disputes between different users of the countryside could be solved by some Whitehall bureaucrat *a priori*. If ever a political issue needed to be left to piecemeal local decision-making and to local politicians rather than national ones, it is the recreational use of the countryside. If it stands by this report, the CPRE should rename itself the Central Planners of Rural England.

20. Green Utopianism*

A code word has crept into environmentalism in recent years: 'values'. Like 'resources', which usually means money (though a friend was recently at a meeting where it turned out to mean toilets), the word is increasingly a euphemism for something else. To celebrate World Environment Day next week, there will be a gathering in London of the Green and the Good (and a few of the Bad, such as me) to discuss 'values'. At issue is the question of whether environmentalism can change people's underlying motives, or just their incentives. In a phrase, must we abandon capitalism to save the planet?

Most radical Greens are in no doubt. They are as revolutionary as any 19th-century anarchist and as impatient to rearrange society. I received through the post the other day a questionnaire about sustainable development, which made it pretty clear what answer the authors expected. 'Which areas of consumption are people most willing to cut back on?', it asked, and 'Which industries, markets and/or products do you think might be targeted for abandonment or scaling down in the cause of sustainability?' Beyond the give-away dictatorial assumption that the world economy is run by central planners, notice the belief that it is consumption, and therefore growth, that is the problem for the environment. If only we could abolish greed, the questionnaire sets out to prove, the environment would be in no trouble at all.

This is classic utopianism. In the Green Utopia people would not try to get richer, but would be happy with what they have. They would not want second cars, or wider roads, or more packaged goods, or chemical detergents: they would just live, growth-less, and be happy ever after. Like most Utopias, this dream is hopelessly naïve about human nature.

Leave aside for the moment the argument that growth has delivered a mostly cleaner world by producing the technologies and the spare wealth and time to clean it up cheaply, and that growth has given us the productivity to feed the population off

---

*Published as 'Going with grain for a capitalist clean conscience' in *The Sunday Telegraph* on 29 May 1994.

less and less land – leaving more and more for conservation. The real problem with the desire to abolish greed is not that it is wrong, but that it is hubristic. Can Greenery really succeed where Marxism failed, and make us less self-interested?

I believe that (successful reproduction and getting into heaven aside) human beings are and always have been driven by three cardinal ambitions – for wealth, for reputation and for status – and that you ignore such facts at your peril. Look no farther than Russia for proof. Marxism fails precisely because it indulges a fantasy that humans will abandon these three and replace them with the greatest good of the greatest number.

In their saner moments, environmentalists understand this perfectly well. When they set out to make people think twice before buying a more thirsty car, or recycle their empty bottles, or tithe some of their income to save rain forests or whales, they may pretend to appeal to our consciences, but they know they are also playing on our vanity. They make it both chic to worry about the rain forest and shameful not to care. They make it politically correct to be Green.

It is not nearly so easy to make Greenery profitable. When a businessman boasts about his company's conscience-spending on nature reserves or research into pollution, he is after brownie points with his shareholders, the media and pressure groups – not profits. On the whole, therefore, environmentalism within a free-market society consists of pitting the brownie points of being clean against the rewards of being dirty. Understandably, environmentalists wish that it were possible to abolish the economic incentives against which they struggle. Hence the daydream about altering the 'values' of society, and inventing a Utopia in which people stop worrying about the next pay cheque and keeping up with the Joneses.

Greens should learn from previous revolutionary movements to work with the grain of society, not against it. Let Greenery be trendy and profitable, not compulsory. Change the incentives, because you will never really change people's 'values'.

21. The Market for Green Ideas*

Here is a new game. Conservation is a highly competitive industry, in which individual organisations compete like companies for market share – except that conservationists measure it in funds, members and publicity, rather than sales. Therefore name the commercial firm each conservation organisation most resembles. There are huge nationalised firms like English Nature (The Post Office?), mature multinationals like the World Wide Fund for Nature (Shell?), big consumer-driven private companies like the Royal Society for the Protection of Birds (Tesco?), fast-growing and aggressive newcomers like Greenpeace (Hanson Trust?), and so on.

As an industry, conservation is in a recession. Shake-ups, redundancies, retrenchments, mergers, crises: all have been announced, leaked or rumoured in the past few months. Greenpeace is having the equivalent of a boardroom battle about how to respond to falling revenues; the British Trust for Conservation Volunteers has had to make redundancies; the Cambridgeshire and Northamptonshire Wildlife Trusts are merging to save costs – and, of course, as in every recession, the government bodies are happily increasing their budgets and their staff numbers regardless.

This recession is caused, ultimately, by the current dip in enthusiasm for green issues that inevitably followed the boom of the late 1980s. But in the resulting shake-out, the ones suffering most are, it seems, the more moderate, local and small-scale: the equivalent of responsible small businesses.

Take the case of the Wildlife Trusts, a loose coalition of county-by-county trusts with 2,000 nature reserves and 250,000 local members. They are the model of a devolved, admin-light, volunteer-led organisation which puts its efforts into actually protecting a rare plant or bog, rather than stuffing the pockets of urban professionals. These trusts are having a difficult time, and they rightly realise that one reason is the success of bigger, more radical and more aggressive campaigning

*Published as 'The best lobby groups come in small packages' in *The Sunday Telegraph* on 23 October 1994.

groups, better suited to the simplicities of tabloid and television journalism.

For instance, in a recent issue of *Natural World*, the trusts' journal, Richard Sharland, who ran the Lancashire Trust until recently, recalls the dilemma he faced when protesters from Earth First! moved into a park managed by the trust to block the building of a motorway. Mr Sharland's trust, when mentioned at all, was accused in the press of both 'resenting' the protesters and 'letting them do its dirty work' simultaneously. Reluctantly accepting the inevitability of the road that the trust had fought at a public inquiry, and trying to negotiate some compensatory conservation work elsewhere, Mr Sharland 'discovered how difficult it is to hold the middle ground'.

The big 'firms', with their bureaucratic structures, cosy lobbying arrangements with government, aggressive tactics and centralised views are driving out the small 'firms' from the conservation scene, to the detriment of conservation. The local trusts are all about putting priorities on issues that matter locally (defending red squirrels in Northumberland's case, for example) and about appealing to those motivated by a love of nature, rather than perpetual moral outrage about supposed crises in the countryside.

The movement is now split between those who want the trusts to become more like their competitors – more 'direct action', less natural history – and those who believe that the trusts should stick to what they are good at: building local bridges with everybody to deliver genuine conservation practically, on the ground. I'm with the latter. It is suicide for Bloggs and Bros to emulate Tesco.   ·

22. Lawyers Take Over Conservation*

Last year the cormorant population of Britain increased by approximately 950 birds. Yet next month a court will sit in solemn session considering hefty affidavits, which aver that the government was unconstitutional in sentencing six cormorants to death on the River Wye during January.

The case has been brought by the Royal Society for the Protection of Birds, which has picked up a habit common among lobbyists in America of suing the Government over the way it enforces its laws. Almost all the American environmental organisations went through a revolution in the 1980s, throwing out the old naturalists and replacing them with litigators and marketing specialists. This gave them the high-profile activism necessary to attract funds to sustain their increasingly heavy administrative budgets. The revolution at the National Audubon Society, the RSPB's equivalent, occurred in 1991 with a whole-sale clean-out of anybody who knew more about birds than the law. 'We want to be Greenpeace,' said one of the new men.

The RSPB's case is that in issuing licences for fishermen on the Wye to kill six cormorants (and similar licences to kill fish-eating ducks called goosanders), the Ministry of Agriculture did not follow the letter of the law. This has won it a judicial review in the High Court, which is to consider both whether the Government disobeyed its own Environmental Information Regulations of 1992 (these, astonishingly, require it to explain its decisions to organisations like the RSPB), and whether the Government's Wildlife and Countryside Act of 1981, under which the cormorant death warrants were issued, is an adequate translation of the 1979 Birds Directive of the European Community.

In contrast to this tortuous legal argument, the underlying issue is simple enough. Cormorants eat fish and have recently moved inland where they are damaging trout, salmon and coarse fisheries. The National Angling Championships, due to be held in Nottinghamshire in September, are in doubt because up to 48

---

*Published as 'What do we want to save: lawyers or cormorants?' in *The Sunday Telegraph* on 13 March 1994.

61

cormorants are eating fish on the lake every day. Therefore, if you are a fisherman, you probably want to shoot some cormorants.

The Government makes it virtually impossible for you to do so. First, you must apply for a licence, providing evidence that the birds are eating fish and doing your business harm. For example, you may have to prove that fewer people are now fishing your stretch of the river because of the declining catch. Then you will be visited by officials from the Ministry to check your claim and to satisfy themselves that you have tried other means of getting rid of the cormorants and failed. And then, if a licence is granted, it will be a very restrictive one. It will say that you cannot shoot a lone cormorant (which would not *encourage les autres*); and it will specify how many you may kill. In the six years up to 1992, 25 licences were applied for, 17 granted, and 84 cormorants were killed. Last year, 53 licences were applied for and 24 granted.

This byzantine procedure is what the RSPB objects to. It would prefer that no licences be given, despite the fact that there is absolutely no conservation issue at stake: the 18,700 British cormorants are swelling their ranks at 5·6 per cent a year (and eating eight tons of fish a year). But instead of saying so, it has gone to court. Government lawyers will therefore, at our expense, be in court arguing not that cormorant killing is being done correctly, but that the Government's procedure for issuing licences is not somehow contrary to some obscure letter of the law.

This is legalism gone mad. The decision to issue a licence to kill a few cormorants is a political decision. It should turn on issues like the number of, and damage done by, cormorants, not on whether some law says exactly what it means or corresponds precisely enough to some sacred Euro-directive. On matters like this, the law should be a slave to policy, not the other way around.

It would be a great shame if the RSPB, which has done so excellent a job over many years running bird reserves, researching bird ecology and giving advice on bird protection, should suddenly turn itself into the Royal Society for the Protection of Lawyers, merely to attract publicity.

23. Jargon-mongers Take Over Natural History*

Two different documents have lain on my desk all week and only when I read one of them carefully did it become apparent that there was a connection between them. One is *Biodiversity Challenge*, an earnest and professional 137-page book on what environmentalists want the Government to do about British biodiversity. The other is a 54-page book published in 1906 called *The British Woodlice*, which I happened upon in a local library.

Both documents are written by naturalists, but how that calling has changed! To be a naturalist in 1906 meant being able to write sentences like:

> 'The antennae are very short and the distal joint of the flagellum is three times the length of the other, while the two together are not as long as the last peduncular joint.'

To be a naturalist in 1994 means being able to write sentences like:

> 'The priorities for biodiversity monitoring in the UK are to establish a framework for biological recording in the UK by implementing the recommendations in phase 1 of the Co-ordinated Council for Biological Recording's (CCBR) report.'

Nowadays, a naturalist needs to know more acronyms than body parts. Yet the Edwardian taxonomist, enthusiastically gathering the microscopic observations of parsons and professors, was laying the foundations for the modern quangologist. Both are concerned with rarity. The woodlice book describes in astonishing detail each of the 17 species of woodlice (those doodlebugs that you find beneath a damp corner of carpet and which roll into little balls when alarmed) that had been identified in Britain. *Biodiversity Challenge* picks up the story 90 years on. It reveals that one of those species, *Armadillidium pictum* (the very species whose peduncular joint is so long), is still rare in its native Westmoreland, Lancashire and Wales. Ergo, says the

---

*Published as 'Forget biology – quangology is the new science' in *The Sunday Telegraph* on 23 January 1994.

modern book, the Government should take its rarity into account when going about its policy-making.

The notion of Westminster discussing whether the upgrading of the West-coast rail line will hurt rare woodlice is not wholly far-fetched. In America, environmentalists use the Endangered Species Act (which also applies to subspecies) in exactly this way to frustrate developers. Next week, the Government is to launch its own biodiversity plan, something it committed itself to do at the Rio de Janeiro summit on the global environment in 1992. This is intended to answer the question so insistently posed by Brazilians and others at Rio: Who are you to tell us to conserve the rainforest? What are you doing about your own environment?

Whatever the Government says, the Greens will not be satisfied (it is not the job of pressure groups to be satisfied). They want, and suspect they will not get, specific commitments to aim for specific targets. For example, *Biodiversity Challenge* would like the Government committed to ensuring that there is at least one pond suitable for great-crested newts per square kilometre of land in areas where such newts might live.

Such targets are useful weapons for Greens, because then they can describe a failure to meet them as a scandal (shock horror: Essex has only one pond per two square kilometres). The Government has already experienced this tactic over deadlines and targets for air pollutants and has no wish to be caught the same way again. So it may content itself with platitudes next week.

There are so many different ways of being rare, as *Biodiversity Challenge*'s fascinating compendium of threatened British species reveals. On the island of Lundy, there is a 'flea beetle' found nowhere else in the world. Lundy also holds the only certain population of the black or ship rat once so common but now driven out by brown rats. Water voles are being driven inexorably towards extinction by introduced mink but in places they are still common. The glutinous snail turned up in a pond in 1989, after being thought extinct for more than 30 years. The stinking hawk's beard has not been seen since the early 1980s. The gannet is numerous and thriving, but two-thirds of all gannets breed in British waters. Barn owls are declining in Britain, but found on almost every continent. The woodlouse, *Armadillidium pictum*, is, and probably always has been, plain scarce – through no fault of mankind's.

24. The Nationalisation of Land*

The Glenfeshie estate, which consists of 42,000 acres of Cairngorm wilderness, may be about to become the latest and largest victim of an intriguing new trend: the collectivisation of land ownership. Until now, most land in this country has belonged to individuals. But it is collective owners – the Government, quangos, pension funds, conservation bodies and companies – that are the future of land ownership. The day of the individual landowner is passing.

The owner of Glenfeshie, a fitted-kitchen entrepreneur who bought the estate in 1988 for more than £2·5 million, is selling because, rumour has it, he is fed up with trying to run an estate overrun with hikers and semi-official busybodies. What's the point, he must have wondered, in owning the land when other people tell him what he can and cannot do? The favourite candidate to buy the estate is the Royal Society for the Protection of Birds.

But even if a private millionaire does buy it, his hands will be tied. Last month there was a revealing letter in *The Scotsman* from Michael Scott of 'Plantlife', who said:

> 'A potential purchaser of the estate might expect for £4-5 million to buy the unfettered right to own and manage the land, but that is far from the case ... He will need extremely broad shoulders because there will be very many people looking over them. I trust the selling agents will make this clear to potential purchasers.'

Translated, this means, 'Let's try to talk down the price so a conservation organisation can buy it'. But what Mr Scott said is absolutely true. Ownership of land no longer means what it used to. When you buy land you acquire rights that have been greatly restricted and circumscribed. If there are buildings, the planners decide what may be done with them down to the last window sash. If there are woods, the Forestry Commission and the planners dictate whether you may fell them and how you must replant them. If there are fields, the Ministry of Agriculture tells

* Published as 'When busybodies lay siege to the gates of the estate' in *The Sunday Telegraph* on 12 June 1994.

you how many of them you may plant each year. If there is a bog, English Nature or its Scottish or Welsh equivalent will designate it as a Site of Special Scientific Interest and give you your orders; if a river bank, expect a call from the National Rivers Authority. There is now no kind of land – except a back garden – that you may do what you like to without permission from a bureaucrat. Only the costs and taxes of ownership are still yours in full.

But, aside from this creeping confiscation of ownership rights by the national government, there has been a steady expansion of collective forms of land ownership: that is, land owned by a corporate, public or voluntary body. The National Trust, the RSPB, the British Rail Pension Fund, farming companies, the Forestry Commission, the Ministry of Defence, local authorities – these are all the great modern landlords, vastly greater than all the dukes and earls put together. I would guess that more than half the land in this country is now in such collective hands. They have one huge advantage: they never pay inheritance tax.

There is nothing automatically wrong with collective land-owners. Many are excellent stewards of the land, just as many individual landowners are incompetent, absentee and thoughtless. The RSPB in particular is an attentive and responsible steward of its reserves. Indeed, what is happening is probably just part of an historical trend, as, a century ago, privately owned firms mostly gave way to limited-liability public companies.

But, as with public companies, something valuable is lost. There is a loss of accountability (try finding out who to blame if something goes wrong), a loss of local control (collective landowners usually take decisions in distant London committee rooms, whereas not all millionaires are absentee), a loss of eccentricity (who ever heard of the National Trust commissioning a folly?), and a loss of continuity (wardens and executives move on or retire after a few years; earls do not).

Many Scotsmen resent the way their mountains became private playthings of the rich in Victorian times. But they should be wary of leaping out of that frying pan into a nationalised fire.

PART VI

BUREAUCRATS

25. Mad Government Extravagance on Motorway Verges*

Those of us who work in the private sector have more and more in common with the subjects of Louis XIV or the Great Inca. Wherever we go, we are affronted by the appalling extravagance of our masters who spend money as if it were water even while we scrimp and save. But whereas once it was aristocrats and monarchs who revelled in largesse at their subjects' expense, now it is government bureaucrats.

These anarchist thoughts are provoked by a stretch of a motorway close to my home. A month ago, there appeared along its edges, beautifully laid and neatly replacing a muddy verge, about half a mile's length of perfect turf – the kind people buy to make instant lawns out of. This had been laid with great care and for the first few days looked lovely and green. Now it is folding back on itself along the joins, yellowing and unhappy. Salt spray after last week's snow is killing it. It will soon be back to mud. Just beside this stretch of new lawn is scattered assorted litter including two discarded milk crates, which have been there for at least a year. The turf layers did not touch them.

Even supposing the Department of Transport gets a discount on its turf, this little exercise in futility will have cost the taxpayer hundreds of pounds – for that stretch alone. Nor is the turf more than the latest sign of absurd extravagance on motorway verges. Last week, two dedicated public servants, decked out in fantastic orange garments, were out strimming the sides of the embankment above the turf, carefully working their way around the many shrubs and trees that cover it.

They were doing a tidy job, but there was only one problem: the grass they were strimming was shorter than the grass on my lawn. They were removing the first half-inch of spring's growth. And these embankments were last strimmed last December, in the middle of winter when grass does not grow.

On the M4 near London, the Department of Transport has even taken to laying great sheets of grey blanket, through which

---

*Published as 'An extravagance that verges on M-way madness' in *The Sunday Telegraph* on 17 April 1994.

the shrubs grow, so that the weeds and grasses are smothered. It all seems to be part of a new attempt to turn the country's motorway embankments into arboretums and weedless borders. More gardening effort is now expended on motorway verges than on the average garden.

I object to this on ecological grounds. Once motorway embankments were left to grow weeds and long grass, which attracted voles and then kestrels (and grew to conceal the relentless litter). It is a long time since I have seen a kestrel hovering over the neatly trimmed lawns of modern embankments. The grass never grows long enough to harbour a vole. Who decided that we needed roadside gardens instead? Some horrendously tidy little Whitehall mind.

But the ecological objection is as nothing beside the financial one. I thought we had a huge government deficit, and had just emerged from a recession. I thought we had been solemnly assured that government spending was being cut to the bone, with great hardship all round, and that was why our taxes had to go up instead. Yet here is a positively Bourbon explosion of unnecessary expense before our very eyes. Or do Treasury ministers never look out of the windows of their official cars?

Of course, were some minister for once to try to stand up to his civil servants and demand a reduced roadside verge garden maintenance budget, the Sir Humphreys would soon outwit him. They would pick the most popular bypass in the country and cancel it, or close a road-safety office or something equally likely to cause real pain. Like all old tricks, it works every time, and you would not see the minister for dust. Then they would get back to issuing more guidance notes on how the latest horticultural advice for motorway embankments is to pull all the shrubs up every two years (they die in two years anyway) and replace them with the latest fume-resistant Tierra del Fuegan variety (only $19·99 a shrub).

That, of course, would be expensive, but no problem. Unlike every other person in the country, but exactly like medieval kings and Inca emperors, public servants can increase their budgets at whim – or by Act of Parliament, which comes to the same thing.

26. Vested Interests and National Forests*

The 'debate' over the privatisation of the Forestry Commission seems to be over. That is, although the Government has said nothing at all, the mediums in the media who interpret to us what is going on in Whitehall are now certain that the Forestry Review Group has decided against privatisation. Flushed with victory, the anti-privatisation lobby now has a new objective. It is demanding that the commission be allowed to buy land. In other words, instead of privatising the Forestry Commission, it wants to nationalise the rest of the countryside.

In an open letter to the Prime Minister, assorted greens, ranging from the Duke of Somerset to David Bellamy, have joined forces to make this request. 'We believe,' they write, 'that the Government should allow the Commission to use any surplus from timber sales and the proceeds from land disposals and commercial recreation ... to purchase as well as sell land.' The same suggestion came out of *Country Life's* recent think-in on the forestry industry.

As self-serving demands for subsidy go, this is pretty rich. At present, the Government roughly breaks even on managing its £750-million-worth of forestry land, but it expects to be making £33 million a year soon, or a 4 per cent return. Since it (or we taxpayers) could probably manage 10 per cent by investing that money elsewhere, it follows that the Government is subsidising the Forestry Commission from public funds to the tune of about £40-70 million. 'Reinvesting the surplus' means keeping that figure high.

I think the Forestry Commission does an excellent job, but that much public money is more urgently needed in the social security budget. The justifications for subsidy are said to be: to maintain public access, to provide recreation facilities, to ensure conservation, to encourage best silvicultural practices and to reduce timber imports. Not one holds water. Public access could easily be guaranteed in privatised woodland by covenant; it does not require nationalisation. The private sector is longing to invest

---

*Published as 'Sell now: why our money should not go on trees' in *The Sunday Telegraph* on 8 May 1994.

in recreational facilities, whereas, like all public sector bodies, the commission is starved of capital. Conservation is ensured by Acts of Parliament that apply with just as much force, or more, to private owners as to public. If the Government wants to subsidise research on silviculture and nesting nightjars, then let it do so and more power to it – but it hardly needs to own the land.

As for the argument that subsidised forestry reduces our trade deficit, even an economic illiterate like me can see the fallacy in this tired mercantilism, a fallacy pointed out by one Adam Smith 200 years ago. We could, if we wanted, reduce our disgraceful dependence on imported bananas by subsidising greenhouses, but it is cheaper to buy foreign bananas and invest the savings in making something at which we have a competitive advantage. Because of geography, we simply do not have a competitive advantage in tree growing. Our summers are too windy and our land is too expensive. Sweden, Russia and Canada are always going to undercut us – just as the Caribbean is always going to grow cheaper bananas. Subsidy will not change that; it will simply draw scarce funds away from better investments.

If they had any force at all, the arguments for public ownership would apply even more to listed buildings and beauty spots. Let us nationalise Chatsworth and the Lake District and Bath to save them for the nation! The anti-privatisation lobby is nothing but the bleat of vested interests: employees who want to remain on the public payroll, environmental organisations which find it more profitable to bully subsidised public bodies than private owners – even landowners and the timber merchants, who greatly enjoy having their main competitor and supplier stuck in the public sector (it is a great myth that businessmen like competition: they prefer monopoly).

The Marxist notion that the state should own the means of production is utterly discredited even in this country. The notion that it should also own all land is exploded by the tragedy of Russia. Yet we are supposed to believe that it makes sense for the Government to own 40 per cent of all woodland. My advice to ministers: continue selling land and do not buy an acre.

27. Ugly Pylons*

Nothing has ever bruised our landscape so badly as electrification. Compared with the untidy ugliness of pylons and wires, the railways and even the motorways are trivial scars. And whereas railways and motorways could not have been built any other way, electricity lines could at least have been buried underground had we been more green-conscious in the 1950s. Should they now be?

This week the Countryside Commission grappled with the issue in a succinct but 'wet' report. Its conclusion was that more 'undergrounding' and rerouting should be the aim of the electricity companies, but that what was needed first were assorted studies and databases on where the visual impact of pylons was worst. Although this sounds sensible, it is an excuse for spending money on studies and consultants rather than action, the hallmark of modern Quangos and environmentalists. Jobs for the boys.

Anybody who has ever travelled through rural America will know how much worse it could be. There, the electric cables are overhead, even in small towns and villages. Such places seem festooned with wire. Here we have at least put most of our low voltage and urban power lines underground. About 60 per cent of our 560,000 kilometres of power lines carrying 11,000 volts or less are already underground.

But whereas the cost of putting a low-voltage line underground is twice as high as putting it on overhead poles, the cost ratio increases to 20 times for the high-voltage, 400,000-volt lines. Pylons are much cheaper than conduits because huge trenches are needed just to cool the high-voltage lines. To a small extent the higher installation cost is offset by lower maintenance costs, but not enough to matter.

So if we are to beautify our countryside, we are going to have to find the money somewhere. There will be a once-a-generation opportunity to do so in the next few years as large parts of the National Grid, much of which was installed in the 1950s, comes to the end of its life. Back then, the taxpayer could be tapped for

*Published as 'Electric supply needs a new line of thought' in *The Sunday Telegraph* on 21 August 1994.

big capital projects because there was not such a vast army of government employees so desperate to spend money on themselves and their consultants as there is today.

Why not link the two problems? Pass a law saying that for every 100 extra employees hired by central government and its quangos, the money must be provided by the Treasury to put one kilometre of high-voltage power line underground (that is, £10 million). That would ensure that current spending could not rise without achieving some useful capital work.

Ironically, the generating industry's dash for natural gas, so deplored by green puritans on the grounds that it is driven by the market, not by a 'strategy', could be a good excuse to tear out lots of pylons. It is cheaper to transport electricity about than coal, which is why so many of our power stations are on the Trent, but it is cheaper to move gas about than electricity. So gas-fired power stations can be closer to where the electricity is needed, requiring fewer pylons.

However, the real problem is not the high-voltage grid, but the much more extensive low-voltage network. With a deep disregard for the landscape and the buildings, we have covered our countryside with lines of wooden poles and wires, about the only advantage of which is that they provide somewhere for swallows to perch at this time of year. Putting them underground costs more, but there is no reason why it should be borne by the taxpayer or by the electricity shareholder.

Whatever happened to local initiative? Negotiate a price from the local electricity company to 'underground' the wires in your local village, form an appeal committee and get fund-raising. If we cannot raise the money in such ways, we obviously do not care enough about the issue.

28. Nitrates and Lunacies*

As government activities go, ordering water companies to spend £160 million to attack a problem that does not exist while blighting the prospects of thousands of small farmers would seem to be foolish, going on criminal. But that is, if anything, a mild description of the British Government's schemes under the European Community's 'Nitrate Directive', to take the force of law some time next year.

The story begins in the late 1970s when medical scientists pinned down the cause of a nasty but non-fatal disease called (its Latin name is indigestible) 'blue-baby syndrome'. The chief cause was a high level of nitrate in the food or drink of the baby. Yet blue-baby syndrome had by then become extremely rare – there has not been a single case in 20 years in this country – and is quite easily cured once diagnosed. It is, literally, nothing to worry about.

About the same time the possibility that stomach cancer might also be promoted by nitrates was raised and then rejected. If there is any link between nitrates and stomach cancer at all, it is either negative (that is, fewer nitrates lead to more cancer) or occurs at unrealistically high levels of nitrates.

Too late came the good news. Rumours of nitrate's ability to kill babies and cause cancer had filtered through the environmental organisations and seeped into the corridors of the Berlaymont. The giant began to twitch; bureaucrats to scribble; and in what for Brussels was but an instant – that is, a decade later in 1991 – a directive was born. It proposed that no source of water in the community should have more than 50 milligrams of nitrate per litre.

This was an absurd figure; not even the ultra-cautious World Health Organisation urged such a maximum. WHO proposed that people should not *on average* drink water with more than 50 mg/l – a very different thing from saying they should never encounter water with that much nitrate. But these were the days of Carlo Ripa di Meana, and the Brussels 'bureaucralariat' was

---

*Published as 'New water law pours money down the drain' in *The Sunday Telegraph* on 2 October 1994.

determined to prove itself greener than thou, to 'lead the world' in standards.

Our Government meekly signed up as usual. Yet not a single expert supported the directive's limit. The Government's own Chief Medical Officer told a House of Lords select committee in 1989 that 100 mg/l was safe. The Parliamentary Office of Science and Technology reported last year that 'at most this might prevent one case of [blue-baby syndrome] every few years' and that allowing up to 100 mg/l would have 'no significant health implications and result in considerable cost savings'. The Royal Commission on Environmental Pollution said in 1992:

> 'We have not been convinced that this strict limit is needed to safeguard health in the UK or any other country with a satisfactory public water supply system.'

Yet 10,000 farmers have just been told they live in 'nitrate-vulnerable zones' and may face strict limits on when and how much they may spread fertiliser or muck on their fields. For marginal dairy and beef farmers such a designation means ruin. The American Department of Agriculture says gleefully that the directive will result in 'very significant falls in output for some livestock products'. Meanwhile, as I learnt from *The Daily Telegraph* last week, our home-grown lettuce producers face extinction under the same rules, because Italian and Spanish lettuces have slightly lower nitrate levels (so the Italians and Spanish want tighter regulations).

The British Government, at last comprehending these arguments, is proposing that the Drinking Water Directive (a different beast) include a more lenient view on nitrate – it is currently up for review. But information takes a long time to travel from the brain of a dinosaur to its tail, and the tail of the bureaucracy continues to press ahead with implementing a rule its head argues against.

29. Save Us from Strategists*

There is no easier way for a politician to get applause than to say 'What we need is a proper strategy . . .', followed by the words 'for the countryside/energy policy/exchange rates', or whatever. Nobody, it seems, is ever against strategies and plans.

Except me. Strategies, to me, embody the fallacy that the world can always be directed from above. Two hundred years of disastrously committing this error, from the mercantilists of the 18th century, via Lenin's five-year plans and Mao's murderous Great Leaps Forward, all the way to the Maastricht Treaty have entirely failed, it seems, to drive home the lesson that democratic, bottom-up, market-led solutions are usually better for more people than *dirigiste* attempts to guess the future.

The latest *dirigiste* idiocy consists of heavy and expensive documents called 'draft local plans' that have been thudding on to desks in the past month. They contain immensely detailed attempts to plan the future of every rural district in the country drawn up by expensive officials and consultants employed by local councils at the instigation of some megalomaniac secretary of state for the environment who has now safely moved on to another job.

These documents suffer not just from the usual flaws of all attempts to plan – for instance, I know that one is already out of date, despite not coming into force for another two years – but they are also extremely sinister. They effectively amount to a vast and yet futile extension of planning policy into new areas.

Take the one in front of me now, drawn up by Conservative-dominated Tynedale Council (all parties are equally guilty here). It shows that if you live, say, in the pretty village of Wall, you are already in a green belt and a conservation area; once the plan comes into force, you will also be in an 'area of high landscape value', a 'commuter pressure area' and something called the 'landscape setting of Hadrian's Wall corridor': three new designations with separate planning policies.

Phew! So Wall is safe, at last. The trouble is, none of the three

---

*Published as 'Save us from cheap talk of the strategists' in *The Sunday Telegraph* on 16 October 1994.

new designations will make the slightest difference either in theory or in practice. Suppose I wanted to buy a plot of land in Wall and cover it with an ugly new development. I would surely never get planning permission, even without all these designations. The case would be treated by the planning committee on its merits.

But even if I were somehow to prevail, it is hard to see what the three new designations would do to stop me, since they merely repeat in a non-statutory way the same principles as the existing designations. So the whole exercise is futile, and a pure waste of taxpayers' money, though great fun for the consultants.

The reason ugly things keep getting built in the British countryside is that such a vastly over-intrusive and detailed planning policy actually plays into the hands of the worst sort of developers: the big ones with deep enough pockets to push on through public inquiries and the rest, while planning officers come down like tons of bricks on poor old Mrs Smith because she tried to put a satellite dish on her Victorian house. In a conservation area, she is breaking the law, even if her neighbour whose house was too ugly to be included in the conservation area, would not be.

Preserve us from more strategies and plans, please. They only encourage despoliation, by making ugly places more developable and therefore more valuable, while punishing those who have looked after landscapes by confiscating their rights to continue doing so.

30. The Mousetrap of Subsidies*

The Labour Party said last week that it would impose a 'Right to Roam' on open country in memory of John Smith, who was a keen bagger of Munros (hills over 3,000 feet tall). This is demagoguery, because the right to roam effectively exists already in Scotland, most of the Lake District and the Pennines. No Munro or fell is out of bounds to hikers. Quite what a formal law would do to improve this situation is unclear, except to annoy landowners.

But that presumably is the point. In almost every respect that you can think of, the nationalisation of the countryside proceeds apace, driven not by ideology but by Parkinson's Law. Every quango finds itself under one-way pressure to increase its own interference in order to 'police' the results of its previous interferences. This has the happy result of increasing its own budget, which as C. Northcote Parkinson so clearly saw, is the way that all bureaucrats express their ambition.

Thus, the 'reform' of the Common Agricultural Policy two years ago made most farming subject to the arbitrary whims of bureaucrats in the Ministry of Agriculture and increased the cost to the taxpayer. Sheep quotas now belong to tenants, who can sell them, leaving the landlord with no right to farm his land at all. He has to buy more quotas from – guess who? – the Government. Yet who paid for the land in the first place and must pay taxes on it if he dies? The landowner. Is he compensated for this confiscation? No.

Likewise, the National Rivers Authority has effectively nationalised the right to fish for trout and salmon in England and Wales, as I discovered when I renewed my fishing licence recently and found it had increased for no good reason from £13·25 to £45 (or by 340 per cent a year). Even if you own a stretch of river bank, and pay steep taxes called sporting rates on it, you may not fish without paying this piece of protection money to the Government. The money is 'needed' to pay for water bailiffs who are hard at work diligently checking that

*Published as 'The mouse trap ensnaring our countryside' in *The Sunday Telegraph* on 18 September 1994.

people have the licences. Let the landowners police their own fishing; the Government does not own the fish.

It is a little known fact that the Forestry Commission has somehow acquired, or granted itself, a share in the ownership of every tree in Britain. If you wish to cut down even a small clump of trees on land that you own, you must now get something called a felling licence from the Forestry Commission, whether the taxpayer's generosity had anything to do with the planting of the trees or not. This licence takes, on average, three months – and rising – to arrive (if at all), after the commission has consulted the local authority (more fingers in pies) and is highly dictatorial. It tells you exactly what mixture of species of trees you must replant the area with.

Countryside stewardship schemes, environmentally sensitive areas and all the rest of the conservation alphabet are being used by bureaucrats as bait to nationalise land. They take money from taxpayers, offer it to landowners like cheese to a mouse, and then snap shut the trap of centralised bureaucratic dictatorship. The aim is entirely defensive. No *nouveau riche* owner would ever get permission to create a Capability Brown landscape today.

So what? If the end-result is less farm fraud, better rivers, protected trees and more conservation, does it matter that a few private property rights (probably acquired by sharp practices in the City or the Civil War anyway) are trampled under foot? Yes, because there are far cheaper ways of achieving better results, through voluntary and market mechanisms. For instance, Sustrans, an organisation devoted to opening bicycle tracks across the country, has negotiated its way over hundreds of miles of towpaths and old railways just by asking nicely. No legal 'right to ride' was demanded; no government bureaucracy invoked to coerce owners.